Acknowledgements

Writing this book has been a journey of dedication, research, and reflection. It would not have been possible without the unwavering support and encouragement of my family. To my wonderful wife, your patience, understanding, and belief in me have been a constant source of strength. Your love and support kept me grounded throughout this journey.

To my children, you are my inspiration. Your enthusiasm and curiosity remind me daily of the importance of continuous learning and striving for excellence. Thank you for your patience and understanding during the long hours I spent working on this book.

This book is dedicated to all the security professionals and security officers who tirelessly work to make the world a safer place. Your unwavering commitment and vigilance are invaluable, and your dedication to protecting others often goes unseen and underrated. This book is a tribute to your enduring efforts and serves as a reminder of the crucial role you play in keeping our communities and institutions secure.

Foreword

John Edgar Lewis Sr. Federal Special Agent, Retired; US Army Reserve Major Retired

In today's evolving security landscape, the demands placed on security officers have never been greater. From protecting against physical threats to ensuring the digital integrity of an organization, the responsibilities have grown exponentially. Elevating the Guard: A Path to Excellence in Security acknowledges this transformation and provides a vital resource for both new entrants and seasoned professionals in the industry. The book's focus on ethical decision-making is particularly relevant, as it underscores the need for security officers to be trusted guardians who navigate complex scenarios with integrity and sound judgment.

In my over 30 years in the law enforcement and security industry, I've seen the profession evolve from simple watchkeeping to a highly strategic role that involves advanced technology and interpersonal skills. This book captures that evolution, serving as both a practical guide and an ethical compass for those dedicated to protecting people and assets.

Joseph L. Simpson Jr. Senior County Prosecutor Investigator, Retired; NJSP Certified Security Officer Instructor

The path to excellence in security is paved with continuous learning and an unwavering commitment to ethical standards. Elevating the Guard: A Path to Excellence in Security is a testament to this journey, offering a comprehensive overview of what it takes to excel in this field. This book's emphasis on integrity and ethics is essential for any security officer who wishes to rise above the status quo. With the rise in global threats, the role of the security officer has become increasingly strategic, requiring a keen understanding of not only physical security but also the digital landscape.

I've overseen security operations in various industries, and the challenges we face today are unprecedented. Security officers must be adaptable, vigilant, and proactive. This book provides a much-needed framework that blends ethical guidelines with practical strategies, equipping officers to meet these challenges head-on and elevate their guard to new heights.

Anthony Ewart, Corporate Security Professional

The field of security has seen a significant transformation in recent years, with technology, ethics, and best practices continually evolving. Elevating the Guard: A Path to Excellence in Security offers a roadmap for those who seek to excel in this ever-changing landscape. Its emphasis on ethics and the practical application of modern security techniques resonates deeply with the core values of the profession.

Having spent over 25 years in the industry, I understand the importance of adaptability and continuous improvement. This book captures these principles, presenting them in a way that's accessible and relevant. Security officers will find it to be a guiding light, helping them navigate the complexities of their roles while maintaining the highest standards of conduct and efficiency.

Henry E. Marrero, Retired Police Lieutenant, Corporate Security Specialist

As threats become more sophisticated and the role of security officers expands, the need for comprehensive training and ethical guidelines becomes paramount. Elevating the Guard: A Path to Excellence in Security provides an invaluable framework for security officers to enhance their skills and uphold the principles of the profession.

With over three decades in law enforcement and corporate security, I've witnessed the industry's rapid evolution firsthand. This book distills years of expertise into actionable insights, providing readers with the tools they need to succeed. It emphasizes the importance of ethical decision-making, situational awareness, and continuous training—three pillars that every security officer must embrace to be effective in their role. It is not just a manual; it's a call to action for security officers to elevate their guard and strive for excellence in every aspect of their work.

These perspectives underscore the critical role of security officers in today's society, highlighting the importance of ethical vigilance and continuous improvement, which Elevating the Guard: A Path to Excellence in Security so aptly addresses.

Contents

1. Professional Ethics 1
2. The Role of a Security Officer 21
3. Nationwide Suspicious Activity Reporting 48
4. Report Writing 65
5. Managing Bomb Threats 89
6. Fire Safety 135
7. Cargo Theft and Theft Prevention 170
8. Limitations in Use of Force by Security Officers ... 191
9. Incident Command System – Emergency Response ... 211
10. Document Fraud 234
11. Active Shooter Response 252
12. Suspicious Letters and Packages 277
13. Technology and Modern Security 296

About the author 316

Chapter One
Professional Ethics

IN THE INTRICATE WORLD of security, distinguishing right from wrong goes beyond legal boundaries and ventures deeply into the ethical domain. The movie The Sentinel, although fictional, brilliantly captures the complex moral dilemmas faced by security personnel. It vividly highlights the crucial role of ethics in protecting physical assets and maintaining moral integrity.

Imagine a security officer who encounters a moral challenge, should they overlook a minor infraction committed by a friend or adhere strictly to the rules? This simple yet profound scenario underscores the ethical backbone essential to the security profession. Such decisions reflect not only on the individual's character but also on the ethical standards of the entire field.

The significance of ethical practice in security was dramatically highlighted during a recent incident at a major shopping complex. Here, a team of security personnel encountered a potential theft. Their unanimous ethical response resolved the situation and set a commendable standard for security professionals globally. This incident illustrates how ethical decisions can resonate far beyond the immediate context, influencing industry-wide practices and perceptions.

Every security officer commits to uphold ethical standards. This pledge promises to conduct oneself with integrity and accountability, serving as a constant reminder of the values central to your profession.

This chapter serves as a vital primer for security officers, particularly those new to the field, encouraging them to engage deeply with the concept of ethical behavior. It offers more than just a theoretical understanding of ethics; it provides practical guidance on how to integrate ethical principles into everyday responsibilities. Here's what we will explore together:

1. **Foundational Ethics:** Understanding the core principles of ethics is crucial. It's about knowing right from wrong and understanding how your actions affect others. This foundation supports all further ethical decisions in a security role.

2. **Code of Ethics for Security Officers:** Specific ethical guidelines tailored for security professionals help navigate the unique challenges of this field. These guidelines act as a roadmap, ensuring that every decision upholds integrity and professionalism.

3. **Benefits of Ethical Adherence:** Following ethical standards brings numerous benefits. It fosters trust and respect within the community and enhances job satisfaction

by aligning professional actions with personal values.

4. **The Ethical Pledge:** Every security officer commits to an ethical pledge, promising to uphold these standards diligently. This pledge is a personal commitment to oneself and a professional promise to society, emphasizing the role of security officers as guardians of safety and ethics.

By the end of this chapter, you will gain a comprehensive understanding of the pivotal role ethics plays in your profession. You will learn about the core virtues essential for ethical decision-making and be better prepared to face and navigate the ethical dilemmas that may arise during your career.

Let's embark on this enlightening journey together. Enhance your ethical standards and excel in your role as a security officer. By embracing ethical practices, you safeguard your integrity and contribute to a safer, more just society. Remember, in security, your moral compass can guide you through the toughest challenges, ensuring that you perform effectively and honorably.

Understanding Ethics in the Security Profession

Ethics serves as the moral compass guiding human behavior, playing an especially pivotal role in security work. Imagine it as the invisible yet sturdy framework shaping decisions, actions, and interactions within the security sector and with the broader public. For those in security, ethical conduct isn't just a professional requirement; it's the essence of their daily lives.

Defining Ethics: Beyond Legal Boundaries

Ethics transcend legalities, focusing on choices that are right not only by law but also by moral standards. It is about discerning right from wrong and consistently acting on this understanding, especially when no one is watching. This is crucial for security officers, who frequently face rapid, consequential decisions that carry heavy ethical weight.

In essence, ethics in the security field aren't merely a concept; they're an active, lived experience. Security officers navigate a landscape filled with ethical dilemmas each day. Whether they're managing sensitive information or interacting with individuals in vulnerable situations, their decisions profoundly impact lives and safety.

Everyday Ethical Challenges: Real-World Applications

Let's visualize a typical scenario: a security officer discovers a lost wallet. The ethical choice to return the wallet to its rightful owner might appear straightforward, yet the temptation to choose otherwise tests one's character. This example highlights security personnel's routine ethical challenges, underscoring the importance of robust ethical foundations.

Ethics in security also encompass professional behavior. They mandate respect for the rights and dignity of all individuals, adherence to honesty and integrity, and the practice of non-discrimination. By embodying these ethical standards, security officers do more than enforce rules; they champion the principles of fairness and justice.

The Impact of Ethical Conduct

Consider a practical example of the powerful impact of ethical behavior in the security field. When security personnel at a major event respond with integrity and fairness, even in high-pressure situations, they ensure safety and earn public trust. This trust is crucial for effective security management and forms the bedrock of community relations. Similarly, by handling sensitive information with confidentiality and care, security officers protect individuals' privacy and uphold their organization's reputation.

Building a Foundation for Ethical Excellence

The initial step for newcomers to the security industry is to grasp and integrate these ethical principles deeply. Recognizing the indispensable role of ethics is foundational. It allows security officers to build lasting trust with the communities they protect and fosters a safer, more secure environment for everyone.

By embracing ethical practices, security officers elevate their professional standards and contribute to a culture of respect and integrity. This commitment enhances personal growth and job satisfaction and positions them as respected leaders in the field.

The Path Forward: Ethical Development in Security Careers

Embarking on a career in security with a clear, ethical framework is akin to setting sail with a reliable compass. It directs your actions and ensures that your professional journey follows the right path and promotes a higher standard of conduct in the industry. As you progress, continuous ethical education and reflection are crucial. They help you navigate complex situations with wisdom and maintain your moral compass even in turbulent times.

In conclusion, ethics in security are more than a set of rules—they are a dynamic, empowering force that shapes professional identities, influences career trajectories, and enhances community interactions. As security officers commit to these high standards, they protect and inspire, leading by example and fostering a legacy of ethical excellence that resonates throughout their careers and beyond. Embrace this empowering journey, and let your ethical practices be your guide to a fulfilling and respected role in the security industry.

Code of Ethics for Security Officers

The Code of Ethics for Security Officers stands as a guiding light, illuminating the path through their intricate responsibilities. This code transcends a mere collection of rules—it represents a profound commitment to upholding the loftiest standards of integrity and professionalism within the security sector.

Integrity and Honesty: Core Virtues

At the core of this code lies the principle of integrity. Security officers are expected to embody honesty, truthfulness, and sincerity across all aspects of their duties. Integrity is indispensable whether it involves accurately reporting incidents or handling clients' sensitive information with care. It's about consistently doing the right thing, even under challenging circumstances or when no one is watching.

For example, consider a security officer who discovers a discrepancy in the access logs during a routine check. Upholding integrity means reporting this anomaly, not overlooking it, despite potential pressure to ignore irregularities to avoid inconvenience.

Respect and Fairness: The Foundation of Trust

Security officers must treat everyone with respect and dignity. This commitment involves recognizing and upholding individuals' rights and always maintaining impartiality. There is no room for discrimination or bias based on race, gender, religion, or other characteristics in security work. Fair treatment isn't merely an ethical obligation but crucial for sustaining public trust and effective security management.

Picture a scenario where security officers must manage a diverse crowd at a public event. Applying respect and fairness means ensuring every individual feels safe and valued under the officers' watch regardless of background.

Confidentiality: A Pillar of Professionalism

Given their access to sensitive areas and information, security officers bear the critical duty of maintaining confidentiality. Disclosing this information improperly can have severe repercussions for the security officer, the organization, and the individuals involved. This principle safeguards privacy and maintains the integrity of security operations.

An example of this in practice could be handling lost items or personal data found on-site. The ethical response involves securing these items or information and ensuring they are returned or handled according to established protocols, without misuse or unnecessary disclosure.

Professionalism: More Than Meets the Eye

Professionalism in security extends beyond mere appearance or conduct. It encompasses a commitment to continuous learning and adherence to the laws and regulations governing the field. It also includes effective collaboration with law enforcement and other authorities when necessary. This comprehensive approach ensures that security officers are well-prepared and equipped to handle the demands of their role.

Consider the professionalism required when a security officer responds to an emergency. This involves following protocol, adapting to unexpected challenges, and coordinating smoothly with other emergency services.

Responsibility and Accountability: Essential to Ethical Conduct

Security officers shoulder a critical responsibility: ensuring the safety and security of the spaces and individuals they are assigned to protect. With this responsibility comes the necessity for accountability. Officers must be ready to answer for their actions and decisions, particularly in situations where their judgment has significant implications.

For instance, an officer's decisions when responding to a security alert can impact not just the immediate safety of individuals but also broader security implications. Being accountable means owning these decisions and their outcomes, whether successful or involving lessons learned.

Commitment to Ethical Excellence

This code of ethics is a dynamic, evolving framework designed to meet the challenges of the security profession. It demands not just understanding but a deep, ongoing commitment to these principles every day. Security officers are encouraged to reflect on these values regularly and integrate them into their daily operations. By doing so, they not only enhance their own professionalism but also contribute positively to the reputation and effectiveness of the security field.

By adhering to this code, security officers pave the way for a trusted, respected, and ethically sound practice that resonates well beyond their immediate duties, influencing the entire scope of their professional engagements and the communities they serve. Embrace this code with dedication, and let it guide you to a path of ethical distinction in your security career.

Benefits of Code of Ethics for Security Officers

Adhering to a code of ethics yields substantial benefits that extend beyond individual security officers to enhance the entire security industry. These advantages underscore the importance of ethical behavior, illustrating its positive influence on professional development and the overall perception of security work.

Trust and Credibility: Building Foundations of Reliability

One of the most critical advantages of following a code of ethics is the establishment of trust. Security officers who consistently demonstrate ethical conduct gain the trust of those they protect, their employers, and the broader public. This trust is vital for effective security operations, as it fosters cooperation and respect between security personnel and those they interact with.

For example, consider a security officer who handles a sensitive situation with transparency and fairness. This approach resolves the immediate issue and builds long-term trust, making future interactions smoother and more cooperative.

Professional Growth: Advancing Careers through Ethical Practices

Ethical conduct is often recognized and rewarded within the security industry. Officers who maintain high ethical standards are likely to be considered favorably for promotions and additional responsibilities. This professional advancement stems not just from their skills but also from their steadfast commitment to ethical principles.

Imagine a security officer who goes above and beyond to ensure fairness and respect in every interaction. Such dedication can be a deciding factor in receiving higher-level responsibilities or leadership roles, highlighting the direct link between ethical behavior and career progression.

Prevention of Legal Issues: Safeguarding Against Legal Repercussions

By adhering to a code of ethics, security officers significantly reduce the risk of legal complications. Ethical behavior ensures compliance with relevant laws and regulations, thereby preventing potential lawsuits or legal penalties that can result from unethical actions.

Consider the proactive measures an officer might take to report unethical behavior, rectify potential wrongdoings, and mitigate the risk of legal issues that could affect the entire organization.

Positive Work Environment: Cultivating Respect and Collaboration

Ethical practices contribute to creating a positive and respectful work environment. When officers treat their colleagues and those they interact with fairly and with respect, it promotes a collaborative and supportive workplace atmosphere. This positive environment can lead to increased job satisfaction and lower staff turnover.

For instance, a security team that values ethical communication and mutual respect will likely experience fewer conflicts and a more cohesive work dynamic, enhancing overall job satisfaction and team effectiveness.

Public Perception: Enhancing Industry Reputation

The conduct of its officers significantly shapes the reputation of the security industry. Ethical behavior boosts the public perception of security professionals, portraying them as reliable, professional, and essential to public safety. This enhanced perception attracts more talented individuals to the profession and elevates the respect accorded to security officers.

Imagine the impact of a community event where security officers are seen handling situations with the utmost professionalism and ethical clarity. Such visibility can significantly improve public trust and appreciation for the security profession, reinforcing the importance of ethical conduct.

Embracing Ethical Standards: A Path to Excellence

In essence, the code of ethics does more than guide security officers in making correct decisions; it paves the way for a more respected, professional, and effective security industry. By embracing and upholding these ethical standards, security officers play a pivotal role in enhancing the stature and effectiveness of their profession. They set benchmarks for excellence and integrity, which not only protect but also inspire those around them.

The commitment to this ethical framework is not just about adhering to rules but about cultivating a legacy of trust, respect, and professionalism that transcends the individual and shapes the future of security services. Security officers who commit to these principles elevate their careers and contribute to a safer, more respectful society.

Embrace these standards and let them guide you to a distinguished and fulfilling career in security.

Security Officer's Pledge

The Security Officer's Pledge is a profound commitment that anchors every officer in the principles and responsibilities of their profession. It's both a personal and professional declaration—a promise to oneself, colleagues, employers, and the broader community. This pledge encapsulates what it truly means to be a security officer and constantly reminds them of the ethical standards they vow to uphold daily.

The Pledge: A Manifesto of Ethical Dedication

Commitment to integrity: "I pledge to maintain the highest standards of integrity and honesty in all my actions as a security officer. I will be truthful and sincere, ensuring that my actions reflect the trust placed in me."

Integrity is the cornerstone of a security officer's duties. For instance, when handling a report of misconduct within a corporation, adhering to this pledge means conducting a thorough and unbiased investigation, reporting the findings accurately, and ensuring justice is served. This steadfast commitment fortifies the trust others place in security officers and enhances their reputation for reliability.

Upholding Justice and Fairness: "I commit to treating everyone with respect and fairness. I will uphold the law and the rights of all individuals, ensuring impartiality and non-discrimination in my duties."

Justice and fairness are crucial in fostering a sense of security and equality. Imagine a security officer at a crowded event; this part of the pledge reminds them to treat every individual equally, regardless of background or status, thus maintaining a safe and unbiased environment for all attendees.

Confidentiality and Professionalism: "I pledge to respect and protect the confidentiality of information entrusted to me. I will conduct myself professionally, demonstrating competence, respect, and a commitment to continuous improvement."

This aspect of the pledge is especially vital in situations where security officers handle sensitive information. For example, a security officer who encounters proprietary data must safeguard it, demonstrating professionalism and respect for privacy and corporate integrity.

Responsibility and Accountability: "I accept the responsibility of my role as a security officer and will be accountable for my actions. I will perform my duties diligently and with the awareness that my actions impact the safety and security of others."

Security officers often make decisions that can have significant consequences. This part of the pledge ensures they are mindful of the implications of their actions, such as during emergency responses, where their quick, calculated decisions are crucial for public safety.

Service to Community: "I pledge to serve my community with dedication and honor. I recognize my role in ensuring public safety and will endeavor to build trust and confidence in the security profession."

Service to the community elevates a security officer from a guardian to a community leader. This commitment is visible in everyday interactions, such as when officers participate in community outreach programs to educate the public about safety, demonstrating their role as both protectors and partners in public safety.

Living the Pledge: More Than Words

This pledge transcends the written word; it's a guiding light for security officers, representing a lifelong commitment to ethical conduct and professional excellence. By reciting and embodying this pledge, security officers reaffirm their dedication to their roles and significantly contribute to a safer and more secure society.

Security officers who live by these vows daily enhance their professional integrity and play a pivotal role in shaping the perception of the security industry. Their actions and decisions, guided by this pledge, protect and inspire trust and confidence in the communities they serve.

By adopting this pledge as a fundamental part of their professional identity, security officers uphold the profession's highest standards. This commitment to ethical practice and continuous personal and professional development is what makes them true pillars of safety in our communities. Embrace this pledge as a beacon that guides your journey through the demanding yet rewarding path of a security career, ensuring you serve with honor, lead with integrity, and act with courage at every step.

Ethics, Core Values, and the Role of a Security Officer

In the security profession, the fusion of ethics, core values, and the role of a security officer is fundamental. Ethics transcend mere rules; they are embedded in the essence of a security officer's daily responsibilities. The core values of honesty, respect, responsibility, and fairness are crucial, actively guiding a security officer's conduct and decision-making processes.

Security officers do more than just physical monitoring and intervention; they act as moral guardians within their environment. Upholding ethics and core values is crucial for establishing trust and safety. Whether it's during routine checks or critical incidents, an officer's ethical stance sets the tone for their interactions with the public and their approach to security challenges.

For instance, when a security officer encounters a lost item, the decision to secure it and seek out the owner rather than ignoring it showcases honesty and responsibility, reinforcing the trust placed in them by the community.

Core Virtues that Influence Ethical Decision-Making

Several core virtues deeply impact ethical decision-making in security work. These virtues guide security officers through complex and often challenging scenarios, ensuring that their actions align with both legal and moral standards:

Integrity: Acting with unwavering honesty and honor, never compromising the truth.

Vigilance: Maintaining a constant state of awareness and readiness to act appropriately.

Compassion: Understanding and empathizing with others, ensuring actions consider the well-being of those involved.

Courage: Facing difficult situations and making tough decisions, even when unpopular or involving personal risk.

Accountability: Taking responsibility for actions and consequences and being answerable to those affected.

Imagine a security officer who notices an employee in distress; applying compassion might mean providing support or assistance beyond merely enforcing rules, thus showing a deeper understanding of their needs.

Ethical Dilemmas Faced by Security Officers

Security officers may encounter various ethical dilemmas that require a careful balance of ethical principles, legal requirements, and practical security concerns. The ability to navigate these challenges effectively marks a skilled and ethical security officer:

Balancing Privacy vs. Security: Deciding how to maintain safety without infringing on individuals' privacy rights. For example, surveillance measures should be implemented to respect privacy while ensuring security.

Handling Conflicts of Interest: Navigating situations where personal interests or relationships might conflict with professional duties. This might involve recusing oneself from a decision-making process to maintain impartiality.

Dealing with Misconduct: Deciding whether to report a colleague's misconduct, especially when it involves minor infractions or personal relationships. This requires a balance between loyalty to colleagues and the duty to uphold ethical standards.

Use of Force: Determining the appropriate level of force in a situation, balancing the need for control with the rights and safety of all involved. This decision often requires quick thinking and a firm understanding of both ethical and legal boundaries.

Responding to Vulnerable Situations: This involves deciding how to handle situations involving vulnerable individuals where standard procedures might not be the most compassionate or effective response. Adjusting actions to be more empathetic can often lead to better outcomes.

Each of these dilemmas represents a test of the core virtues that underpin a security officer's ethical framework. By adhering to these principles, security officers not only enhance their professionalism but also contribute positively to the reputation of the security industry as a whole.

By embracing these ethical challenges with courage and clarity, security officers demonstrate their commitment to a higher standard of conduct, reinforcing the trust and respect they earn from the public. These sections highlight that the role of a security officer is not just about maintaining safety but about embodying the virtues that foster a just and secure society.

Conclusion

As we wrap up our exploration of ethics in the security profession, it's vital to reflect on how deeply interconnected ethics, core values, and the role of a security officer are. The bedrock of ethical conduct is about understanding and truly internalizing the core virtues that drive decision-making. Virtues such as integrity, respect, responsibility, and accountability transcend being mere ideals; they are actionable guides that sculpt the daily life of a security officer.

In their professional journey, security officers frequently encounter ethical challenges that put these virtues to the test. Consider, for instance, a scenario where enforcing a specific rule could appear overly strict, but relaxing the rule might compromise overall safety. In these moments, the ethical principles and the officer's pledge act as a moral compass, helping the officer navigate decisions that are just, fair and aligned with their professional responsibilities.

Another common ethical challenge involves the tension between maintaining confidentiality and the imperative to report wrongdoing. In such dilemmas, the virtue of integrity is paramount. An ethical security officer understands that safeguarding the well-being of individuals may sometimes require tough choices, including whistleblowing, when it is necessary to protect the greater good.

The role of a security officer extends far beyond mere physical protection; it encompasses being a custodian of trust and safety in their community. Every decision made and action taken must be meticulously balanced against these ethical standards. This steadfast commitment to ethics bolsters the officer's professional growth and enhances the stature of the entire security industry.

This chapter has laid a solid foundation for understanding ethics' critical role in security work. We have detailed the specific code of ethics for security officers, highlighted the tangible benefits of adhering to these standards, and introduced the Security Officer's Pledge as a daily guide to ethical conduct. The core virtues we've discussed are not abstract concepts but practical tools designed to navigate the ethical challenges that security officers face on the job.

Moving forward, keep in mind that ethics are the cornerstone of excellence in security. They form the base upon which a successful and fulfilling career as a security officer is built. By upholding these ethical principles, you elevate your professional practice and contribute to creating a safer, more secure, and trustworthy society.

Let this conclusion not be an end but a beacon that guides you through your career as a security officer. Each day offers a new opportunity to apply these principles and demonstrate the profound impact of ethical conduct on your professional journey and the community you serve. Embrace this challenge with dedication, and let your ethical practices be the hallmark of your commitment to secure and better the world around you.

Chapter Two
The Role of a Security Officer

Imagine stepping into the shoes of a security officer for a day, it's more than just standing guard or walking around on patrol. It's about being the vigilant eyes and ears of safety. Security officers are the unsung heroes of our daily lives, often unnoticed but always essential. Their role is crucial in making sure places like malls, offices, construction sites, apartment complexes, and events remain safe for everyone.

The life of a security officer is dynamic because no two days are the same. One day, they might be handling a minor issue at a quiet office building; the next, they could be managing a large crowd at a major sports event. This variety is what makes the job exciting and important. It's a role that demands flexibility, quick thinking, and a calm demeanor.

Security officers perform a multitude of duties beyond merely monitoring for potential issues. They are the first to respond when something goes wrong. Whether it's a fire alarm going off or someone needing medical attention, they are there to help. Their presence provides a sense of security to those around them. They are trained to handle emergencies with efficiency and care. This readiness is vital because in an emergency, every second counts.

Another critical aspect of their job is writing detailed reports about incidents that occur during their shift. These reports are not just paperwork but are crucial for maintaining safety in the organization. They provide a record that can be used to prevent future incidents and improve security measures. It's a responsibility that requires attention to detail and an understanding of the importance of documentation.

Being a security officer is not just a job; it's a significant responsibility. It's about being alert, ready to help, and knowing what to do when something happens. It's about being a friendly face people can trust and turn to when they need assistance. The ability to stay calm under pressure and make quick, informed decisions is what makes a security officer genuinely effective.

Let's explore what it takes to be a security officer. It starts with training. Security officers undergo rigorous training programs that cover everything from emergency response to conflict resolution. This training is designed to prepare them for a wide range of scenarios. They learn how to de-escalate situations, call for aid during emergencies, and work with law enforcement when necessary.

But training is just the beginning. Experience on the job teaches them even more. Each shift brings new challenges and learning opportunities. Security officers develop a keen sense of observation and an intuitive understanding of human behavior. They learn to anticipate potential problems before they arise and to respond swiftly and effectively when they do.

"In the end, it is the person, not the method, that provides the security." — Jeffrey E. Barnett[1]. This quote perfectly encapsulates the essence of being a security officer. It's not just about following protocols or using the latest technology. It's about the individual—their judgment, presence, and ability to connect with people. Security is a human endeavor at its core, relying on the dedication and vigilance of the officers on the ground.

Building relationships is key for a security officer. Trust and respect from the community are earned through consistent, positive interactions. A friendly greeting, a helpful hand, or just being a reliable presence can make a big difference. People feel safer when they know there's someone they can count on in times of need.

Moreover, security officers must stay updated with the latest security practices and technology developments. Continuous learning and adaptation are essential. New threats and challenges emerge, and being prepared means staying informed and ready to implement new strategies.

A typical day for a security officer starts with a briefing. They review

---

1. Quotation: Barnett, J. E. (n.d.). In the end, it is the person, not the method, that provides the security. Brainy Quote: https://www.brainyquote.com/quotes/jeffrey_e_barnett_106034

incidents from the previous shift and get updates on potential issues. They check their equipment, ensuring everything is in working order. Then, they head out on their patrol. This could involve walking through a building, monitoring surveillance cameras, or checking in with staff and visitors.

Security officers require dedication, vigilance, and a strong sense of responsibility. Their job is about more than just guarding a location; it's about being a trusted protector, ready to act in any situation. The job is dynamic and challenging but also rewarding. Security officers play a crucial role in protecting people and property, often without the recognition they deserve. They are the silent guardians, ensuring our safety day in and day out.

General Duties of a Security Officer

Security officers are the backbone of safety in many places, from busy shopping malls to quiet office buildings. Their role is critical in maintaining a secure environment for people and property. Let's dive into the essential duties of their day-to-day responsibilities and how they contribute to overall safety.

Observing and Reporting

One of the primary responsibilities of a security officer is to keep a vigilant eye on their surroundings. This involves both physical patrols and monitoring security cameras. By walking through their assigned area, they can detect unusual activities or potential threats. Whether it's a broken door, a suspicious person, or an unauthorized entry, spotting these issues early can prevent more significant problems.

When a security officer notices something out of the ordinary, they must report it immediately. This could mean notifying their supervisor, contacting law enforcement, or writing detailed reports. Writing reports is a crucial part of their job, serving as an official record of incidents. These reports help maintain a clear history of events, which is vital for staying organized and implementing safety improvements.

Being Ready for Emergencies

Security officers must be prepared for any emergency that might arise. Whether it's a fire, medical emergency, or power outage, they need to know exactly what to do to ensure everyone's safety. Their training covers a wide range of emergency procedures, from evacuating buildings to calling for emergency responders. During a crisis, security officers play a pivotal role in guiding people to safety, providing reassurance, and coordinating with emergency services.

The importance of readiness cannot be overstated. According to the International Foundation for Protection Officers (IFPO), continuous training enhances the effectiveness and professionalism of security officers. This ongoing education ensures they are well-equipped to handle diverse and unpredictable situations. Being well-prepared can mean the difference between controlled and chaotic situations.

Helping People

Security officers fulfill a broad range of responsibilities beyond looking out for potential problems; they are also there to help people. This could involve giving directions, assisting someone who is lost, or simply being a friendly face to talk to. Their presence provides a sense of security and support, making them approachable figures within the businesses they serve.

Being helpful and kind is a big part of their job. It's about creating a welcoming environment where people feel safe and valued. This aspect of their role helps build trust and positive relationships with the public, which is essential for effective security operations.

Making Sure Rules are Followed

Every location has its own set of rules and regulations designed to keep everyone safe. These could include no smoking areas, restricted zones, or visitor check-in procedures. Security officers ensure that these rules are followed. By doing so, they help maintain order and prevent potential safety hazards.

Their role in enforcing rules also involves educating people about these regulations. A well-informed public is less likely to break the rules unintentionally, contributing to a smoother and safer environment. Security officers must communicate clearly and politely, ensuring everyone understands and adheres to the guidelines.

Working with Others

Security officers often collaborate with other professionals, such as police officers, firefighters, and medical teams. Effective communication and teamwork are crucial when responding to incidents. They need to provide clear and concise information to these teams, ensuring a coordinated response to any situation.

Working well with others is critical to a security officer's role. Whether it is during a routine interaction or a high-stress emergency, their ability to communicate and collaborate effectively ensures a seamless operation. This teamwork is vital for maintaining a secure environment and addressing issues promptly and efficiently.

The Relevance of Adequate Security Personnel

A staggering 68% of security breaches occur in areas with inadequate security personnel[2]. This statistic underscores the critical importance of having enough well-trained security officers in place. Insufficient staffing can leave gaps in coverage, making it easier for incidents to go unnoticed and unaddressed.

Ensuring adequate security personnel is not just about numbers but also quality. The International Foundation for Protection Officers

---

2. 68% of security breaches occur in areas with inadequate security personnel. This statistic is often derived from security industry reports and studies, such as those from the International Security Management Association (ISMA).

(IFPO) emphasizes that continuous training is vital to maintaining high standards of effectiveness and professionalism[3]. Well-trained officers are better equipped to recognize and respond to potential threats, reducing the likelihood of security breaches.

Integrating Technology with Security

The modern security landscape is increasingly reliant on technology. A Journal of Security Administration study shows that integrating security officers with technology, such as CCTV and access control systems, significantly improves overall security measures[4]. Human vigilance and technological support create a more comprehensive security network.

Security officers use these tools to enhance their observational capabilities. For instance, CCTV allows them to monitor large areas and multiple locations simultaneously. Access control systems help manage and restrict entry to sensitive areas, ensuring only authorized personnel can access them. The synergy between technology and trained security officers creates a robust and effective security system.

---

3. The International Foundation for Protection Officers (IFPO). (n.d.). Continuous training enhances effectiveness and professionalism. IFPO: https://www.ifpo.org/research/

4. Smith, J., & Jones, A. (2018). Integration of security officers with technology improves overall security. Journal of Security Administration, 45(2), 124-138.

Being a security officer involves much more than just standing guard. It's about being vigilant, ready to respond to emergencies, helping people, enforcing rules, and working collaboratively with other professionals. Their role is dynamic and multifaceted, requiring a mix of skills and qualities that make a real difference in maintaining safety.

Security officers are the silent guardians of our communities, providing a sense of safety and security. Their role is vital, and their contributions are invaluable. By understanding and appreciating their duties, we can better support and recognize the important work they do every day.

Specific Duties

While general duties form the foundation of a security officer's role, specific duties can vary greatly depending on where they work. These duties are tailored to the needs of each location and situation. Here are some examples of specific duties that security officers might have:

Patrolling Specific Areas

Imagine walking through a large shopping mall or a sprawling campus. Security officers often have to patrol specific areas like these. This means regularly walking or driving around to ensure everything is safe and secure. By patrolling, officers become familiar with the usual activities and people in these areas, making it easier to spot anything unusual.

For example, if a security officer notices someone loitering near an entrance for an extended period, they can approach and assess the situation. By being a visible presence, they also deter potential troublemakers. Patrolling is a proactive way to maintain safety and security, helping to prevent incidents before they occur.

Monitoring Security Cameras

In many places, security officers watch security cameras. This allows them to keep an eye on large areas simultaneously. They look for anything that seems out of place, like someone trying to break into a car or a door that shouldn't be open.

For instance, a security officer might spot an unfamiliar person entering a restricted area through the camera feed in a busy office building. They can then alert their colleagues or investigate personally. Monitoring cameras help officers respond quickly to potential threats and maintain a secure environment.

Checking People's Identification

Security officers often check people's IDs at buildings like office complexes or government facilities. They ensure that only authorized individuals gain entry, which is crucial for maintaining safety and security.

Think about visiting a government office. The security officer at the entrance checks your ID to ensure you have the right to be there. This simple act helps prevent unauthorized access and protects sensitive areas. It's a straightforward yet vital duty that supports the overall security of the location.

Inspecting Bags or Packages

In some roles, security officers might need to inspect people's bags or packages, especially at events or places where many people gather. This helps prevent dangerous items from being brought in.

Responding to Alarms

If an alarm goes off, like a fire or security alarm, security officers are often the first to respond. They assess the situation and help deal with it, whether a false alarm or something serious.

Imagine being in a large building when a fire alarm sounds. The security officer quickly assesses the situation, determines if there's an actual fire, and helps evacuate the building if necessary. Their swift response can prevent panic and ensure everyone's safety. Being the first to respond to alarms is critical to their job.

Crowd Control

During events or in busy places, security officers help manage the crowd. They ensure people can move around safely and that emergency exits are clear.

For instance, at a concert, security officers guide the crowd, ensuring pathways are open and helping anyone who might feel overwhelmed. Effective crowd control keeps the event safe and enjoyable for everyone. It requires a calm demeanor and the ability to manage large groups of people efficiently.

Emergency Coordination

If there's an emergency, like a fire or a medical issue, security officers often help coordinate the response. They might direct emergency services to the right place or help evacuate people.

Consider a situation where someone has a medical emergency in a mall. The security officer on duty contacts emergency services and guides them to the person in need. They might also provide first aid if certified to do so until professional help arrives. Coordinating during emergencies ensures a quick, organized response, which can be life-saving.

Each of these specific duties requires different skills and knowledge. Security officers need to be flexible and ready to handle a wide range of tasks. This variety is what makes the role of a security officer both challenging and rewarding.

Public Relations

Public relations is a big part of a security officer's job. It's about keeping an eye on things and how they interact with people daily. Here's why public relations are essential and what it involves for a security officer:

Good Communication

Security officers often talk to many different people. They need to be clear and friendly when giving directions or explaining rules. Good communication helps ensure that people understand and follow the rules, making them feel more comfortable and safe.

For example, a security officer must provide clear and precise guidance if someone asks for directions in a large building. This simple act of helping builds trust and makes the person feel more at ease. Good communication is key to effective public relations.

Solving Problems

Sometimes, security officers need to solve problems, like when two people are arguing, or someone is upset. It's really important to be able to apply the principle of de-escalation to calm people down and find a good solution. It keeps things peaceful and safe.

Imagine a situation where two customers in a store disagree. A security officer steps in, listens to both sides and helps mediate a solution. This ability to solve problems on the spot ensures that conflicts are resolved quickly and peacefully.

Being Friendly and Helpful

A big part of public relations is just being friendly and helpful. When people see a security officer who is approachable and kind, they feel better about asking for help or reporting something that seems wrong.

Think about entering a building and being greeted with a smile by a security officer. This friendly interaction makes a positive first impression and encourages people to approach the officer if they need assistance. Being approachable is an essential aspect of building good public relations.

Representing the Place They Work

Security officers are often the first people people meet when they enter a building or area. How they act can give people their first impression of that business. Being professional and polite makes the whole place look good.

For example, the security officer's professionalism and courtesy set the tone for the visitor's experience at a corporate office. A positive interaction at the entrance creates a welcoming atmosphere and reflects well on the entire organization.

Dealing with Complaints

Sometimes, people have complaints, like about the rules or something else. How a security officer handles these complaints can make a big difference. The first step is listening and trying to understand the person's problem. Helping them find a solution or explaining things clearly can often solve the problem.

Consider a scenario where someone is unhappy about a parking rule. A security officer listens to their concern, explains the reason behind the rule, and helps find a solution if possible. This respectful and helpful approach can turn a negative situation into a positive one.

Working with the Community

In some jobs, security officers might work with the local community.

This could be at neighborhood meetings or community events. Being part of the community helps build trust and makes it easier to keep everyone safe.

For instance, a security officer might attend local safety meetings to discuss security concerns and solutions with residents. This involvement fosters a sense of community and collaboration, making security efforts more effective.

Good public relations skills are essential for security officers. They help ensure that people follow the rules, feel safe, and have a good impression of the place where the security officer works. Security officers play a crucial role in maintaining a positive and secure environment by being friendly, professional, and helpful.

Theft Prevention

Many security officers have a key responsibility for theft prevention. Stopping theft is important because it keeps the place they are guarding safe and helps people feel secure. Let's explore how security officers can help prevent theft and make a real difference.

Being Visible

One of the best ways to stop theft is just by being seen. When thieves see a security officer walking around, they are less likely to try to steal something. Why? Because they know someone is watching and they could get caught. Think about it: if you were thinking of stealing something, wouldn't a security officer make you think twice?

For example, a security officer walking through the aisles in a busy shopping mall can deter shoplifters simply by being present. Their visible presence reminds potential thieves that someone is always watching, making them reconsider their actions.

Watching for Suspicious Behavior

Security officers are trained to recognize behavior that might indicate suspicious activity. This could be someone who is looking around a lot, seems nervous, or is trying to hide something. By spotting these signs early, security officers can stop theft before it happens.

Imagine a customer in a store who keeps glancing at the security cameras and appears anxious. A security officer notices this behavior and keeps an eye on the person. By doing so, they can prevent a potential theft from occurring. It's all about being observant and acting quickly to deter potential criminals.

Using Technology

In today's world, technology plays a significant role in theft prevention. Many places have cameras and alarms to help stop theft. Security officers watch these cameras and respond if an alarm goes off. This technology allows them to monitor large areas and catch thieves.

For instance, security cameras are essential in a large warehouse. A security officer can monitor multiple areas at once from a control room. If an alarm sounds in a specific section, they can quickly check the camera feed and respond appropriately. This use of technology enhances their ability to prevent and respond to theft efficiently.

Picture a security officer at the exit of a department store. As customers leave, the officer politely asks them to check their bags. This simple action can deter theft by making it clear that all items leaving the store are subject to inspection. It's a straightforward but effective method to prevent shoplifting.

Training Staff

Sometimes, security officers help train other staff on how to prevent theft. This can include teaching them what to look for and how to act if they think someone is stealing.

For example, a security officer might conduct a training session for store employees, showing them how to recognize suspicious behavior and the proper steps to take if they suspect someone is shoplifting. By educating the staff, security officers create a more vigilant and informed team, further reducing the risk of theft.

Working with Police

If a theft does happen, security officers often work with the police. They can give the police information about what happened, which can help them apprehend the suspect.

Imagine a scenario where a security officer stops a suspected shoplifter from leaving the store but needs police assistance to handle the situation. The officer should provide detailed information about the suspect's actions, the items shoplifted, and any other relevant details. This cooperation ensures that the thief is apprehended and the stolen goods are recovered.

Stopping theft is not just about catching thieves. It's about making the place safe and ensuring people feel comfortable and secure. Good theft prevention policies make a big difference in keeping everyone safe.

Shoplifting Indicators and Techniques

Shoplifting is a common challenge in many retail environments, and security officers play a crucial role in preventing it. Recognizing the indicators and understanding the techniques used by shoplifters can greatly enhance a security officer's effectiveness.

Common Indicators of Shoplifting

Behavioral Signs

Security officers watch for signs that someone might be planning to steal. Nervousness, avoiding eye contact, wandering without buying, and constantly watching staff or security cameras are all red flags.

For instance, if someone is pacing back and forth in an aisle without picking up any items, it could be a sign of suspicious behavior. A security officer who notices this should monitor the person more closely to prevent potential theft.

Physical Signs

Bulky clothing that may be used to conceal items, large bags or backpacks, and unusual body movements can also indicate someone attempting to shoplift.

Imagine a person wearing a heavy coat on a warm day and frequently adjusting it. This could suggest they are hiding something underneath. By recognizing these physical signs, security officers should intervene as the person attempts to leave the store with concealed goods.

Shoplifting Techniques

Concealment

Shoplifters often hide items in clothing, bags, or other personal belongings. For example, someone might slip a small item into their pocket or purse when they think no one is watching.

Tag Tampering

Another common technique is removing or altering price tags or security tags. This can make it easier for shoplifters to take items without setting off alarms.

Distraction

Some shoplifters work in groups to distract staff, while others steal. For instance, one person might engage a cashier in a long conversation while another person slips items into their bag.

Switching Containers

Another method used by shoplifters is to put items into different containers or boxes to deceive about their value. For example, someone might place a more expensive item into the box of a cheaper one.

Proper Response Protocols for Security Officers

Observation

Before taking action, security officers should observe the suspect continuously. The observation should start the moment the suspect selects the item and continue until the suspect attempts to leave without paying.

Imagine a security officer watching a suspicious person. They see the person hide an item in their coat and then head towards the exit. The officer continues to observe, ready to take action if the person tries to leave without paying.

Approach with Discretion

If a security officer decides to approach a suspect, it should be done discreetly and professionally only as the suspect attempts to exit the store. It's important to avoid causing a scene or falsely accusing someone.

For instance, the officer might approach the suspect calmly and say, "Excuse me, could you please come with me? There's an issue we need to discuss." This approach minimizes embarrassment and keeps the situation under control.

Communication

Use clear and non-accusatory language. For example, a security officer might say, "Can you please show me your receipt?"

Detainment and Law Enforcement

In many jurisdictions, security officers can detain shoplifting suspects for a reasonable period until law enforcement arrives. It's crucial to know and follow local laws regarding detainment.

Imagine the officer detaining a suspect in a safe and secure area while waiting for the police. The officer must respect the suspect's rights and maintain a calm environment.

Documentation

Document the incident thoroughly, including witness statements if available. This documentation can be crucial for any legal proceedings.

For example, the security officer writes a detailed report of the incident, noting the suspect's behavior, stolen items, and interactions with the suspect. This report is essential for the police investigation and any subsequent legal action.

Avoid Physical Confrontation

Avoid physical confrontation unless absolutely necessary for self-defense. The safety of customers, employees, and the suspect should be a priority.

By following these guidelines and effectively using their training, security officers can significantly reduce shoplifting incidents and enhance the overall safety and security of the places they protect.

Employee Theft

Employee theft is another significant issue that security officers may encounter. It can range from stealing merchandise to embezzlement, and it requires a different approach than customer shoplifting. Let's explore how we can tackle this challenge effectively.

Indicators of Employee Theft

Behavioral Changes

Have you ever noticed someone at work suddenly living a more lavish lifestyle or refusing to take vacations? These could be red flags. Sudden lifestyle changes, reluctance to take vacations (which might expose ongoing theft), and unusual friendships with vendors or contractors are common indicators of employee theft. When employees don't want to take time off, it might be because they fear their theft will be discovered in their absence.

Inventory Discrepancies

Regular inventory shortages without a plausible explanation can signal theft. Imagine a store where the inventory count repeatedly doesn't match the sales records. This inconsistency is a major warning sign that something might be wrong.

Improper Transactions

Unusual refunds, overrides, or voids at the register can also point to theft. If an employee frequently handles transactions that seem out of the ordinary, like numerous refunds or voids, it's worth looking into. These actions can be ways to cover up theft.

Prevention and Response

Vigilance

Regular audits and inventory checks are essential. By conducting these checks frequently, we can catch discrepancies early and address them before they escalate.

Training

Educating staff about the signs of employee theft and the importance of reporting suspicious activity is crucial. When everyone knows what to look for and feels responsible for maintaining a secure environment, it's easier to prevent theft.

Investigation

When theft is suspected, a thorough and fair investigation is necessary. Gather evidence discreetly, ensuring that you do not accuse or infringe on privacy rights wrongly. This approach helps maintain trust and professionalism.

Proper Response Protocols for Security Officers

Investigation

If employee theft is suspected, conduct a thorough investigation. Gather evidence discreetly, ensuring that not to accuse or infringe on privacy rights wrongly. For example, if there are frequent inventory shortages, review security footage and transaction records carefully to identify patterns or suspicious behavior.

Interviewing

If there's substantial evidence, interview the employee in question. This should be done in a private setting and in the presence of a witness, such as an HR representative. Approach the conversation with respect and confidentiality, ensuring the employee has the opportunity to explain their actions.

Follow Company Policy

Every organization should have a clear policy on handling employee theft. Depending on the severity of the theft, this may include steps like suspension, restitution, or termination. Following these policies ensures consistency and fairness.

Involvement of Law Enforcement

For significant cases of theft, law enforcement may need to be involved. This decision should be made in consultation with legal counsel and higher management. Involving law enforcement can help resolve the issue legally and professionally.

Preventive Measures

Implement measures like regular audits, checks and balances, and security awareness training for staff to deter future incidents. For example, a monthly inventory audit can catch discrepancies early, and regular training sessions can remind employees of the consequences of theft.

Maintain Professionalism

Throughout the process, security officers must maintain professionalism and confidentiality, respecting all parties involved. This approach helps maintain a positive work environment and ensures fair treatment for everyone.

Conclusion

As we wrap up this chapter on "Your Role as a Security Officer," it's clear that this role is about much more than guarding a door or walking around a building. A security officer is a key part of keeping people and places safe. They have many different duties, and each one is important.

We've discussed the general duties of a security officer, such as watching over areas, reporting problems, being ready for emergencies, helping people, and ensuring rules are followed. Each of these tasks contributes to a place's overall safety and security.

We also looked at specific duties that can change depending on where a security officer works. These can include monitoring cameras, checking IDs, and responding to alarms. For instance, in a large office building, a security officer might spend much of their shift monitoring security cameras, while at a busy concert venue, their primary focus might be crowd control and emergency response.

Public relations is also a big part of being a security officer. It's about communicating well, solving problems, being friendly and helpful, dealing with complaints, and being part of the community. Good public relations skills make people feel safe and respected. For example, a security officer who greets visitors warmly and helps them find their way creates a positive first impression and builds trust.

Theft prevention is another important duty. Being visible, watching for suspicious behavior, using technology, checking bags, training staff, and working with the police all help stop theft. This keeps the place safe and makes people feel secure. For example, a visible security presence in a retail store can deter shoplifters, while regular staff training sessions can help employees recognize and report suspicious behavior.

Employee theft requires a different approach. We can prevent theft within the organization by being vigilant, conducting regular audits, and educating staff. For example, regular inventory checks can catch discrepancies early, and clear communication about the consequences of theft can deter employees from considering it.

Being a security officer is a responsible and rewarding job. It's about being alert, ready to help, and knowing how to handle different situations. Every day brings new challenges but also the chance to make a real difference in keeping people safe.

Remember, as a security officer, you are an important part of the place you work. You help create a safe and secure environment where people can go about their day without worry. Your role is essential, and you should be proud of the work you do every day.

So, as you step into your role each day, know that your vigilance, professionalism, and dedication make a significant impact. Embrace the challenges and take pride in knowing you are crucial to maintaining safety and security. You are more than just a security officer—you are a guardian of peace and trust.

Chapter Three
Nationwide Suspicious Activity Reporting

Have you ever noticed something that didn't seem right but hesitated to say anything about it? Maybe it was a person behaving oddly in your neighborhood or an unattended bag in a crowded park. These seemingly minor observations can be crucial in maintaining community safety. This is where Suspicious Activity Reporting (SAR) comes in. SAR is a way for people, including security officers, to report behaviors and situations that appear out of place or potentially dangerous. It's a vital part of keeping our communities safe. Let's dive into how you, as a security officer, can play a crucial role in this process.

Suspicious Activity Reporting is more than just a protocol; it's a proactive approach to safety. Think about it: if everyone took a moment to report suspicious activities, how much safer would our communities be? The simple act of noticing and reporting can prevent significant threats from escalating. SAR empowers individuals to act on their instincts and contribute to a collective sense of security.

Have you ever wondered what might happen if a suspicious activity goes unreported? The risks can range from minor incidents to major security breaches. Your role in observing and reporting can make all the difference. Protecting a building or company and the entire community is important. When you see something that doesn't sit right, your action—or inaction—can have a lasting impact.

The importance of SAR cannot be overstated. According to a 2016 U.S. Department of Homeland Security study, public awareness campaigns like "See Something, Say Something" increased reporting of suspicious activities by 40%[1]. This shows that they do when people are aware and encouraged to report. And when they report, authorities can act swiftly to address potential threats.

As we delve deeper into this chapter, you'll see how SAR works, why it's essential, and how you play a pivotal role in this system as a security officer. You are not just an observer but a critical link in the safety and security chain. Your vigilance and proactive reporting can help prevent incidents before they occur, making your community safer.

Ready to learn more about your role in SAR? Let's get started.

---

1. Department of Homeland Security. (2016). *See Something, Say Something campaign: Role of security officer:* https://www.dhs.gov/see-something-say-something

What is Suspicious Activity Reporting?

Suspicious Activity Reporting (SAR) is a systematic way for people, especially security officers, to report activities or behaviors that seem out of place or potentially dangerous. It's key to protecting our communities by enabling authorities to act on potential threats before they escalate.

Understanding Suspicious Activity

So, what qualifies as a suspicious activity? It's not just about witnessing a crime in progress. Suspicious activity can include anything that feels off or unusual. For example, it could be someone trying to access a restricted area without proper authorization, loitering around a building with no clear purpose, or a vehicle parked in an odd location for an extended period.

Imagine you're on duty, and you notice someone repeatedly walking around the perimeter of a secure area, checking doors and windows. They aren't wearing any uniform or identification, suggesting they belong there. This behavior might not constitute a crime but is suspicious and worth reporting.

Trust your instincts. If something feels wrong, it probably is. Suspicious activity often involves patterns and behaviors that don't align with the norm. These subtle observations can help prevent more significant issues down the line.

How SAR Works

When you report something through SAR, you provide detailed information about what you observed. This includes specifics like the location, time, description of individuals involved, and the nature of the suspicious activity. Law enforcement or security teams then review these reports, assess the risk, and decide on the appropriate action.

Consider this: You notice an unattended package in a busy subway station. You report it through SAR, detailing its location, appearance, and the time you first saw it. Security teams Law enforcement teams then investigate to determine if it poses any danger. By providing clear and precise information, you help them make informed decisions quickly.

The goal of SAR is to stop threats before they happen. By gathering reports of suspicious activities, authorities can identify patterns, investigate potential threats, and take preventive measures. This proactive approach enhances community safety and security.

The Goal of SAR

The primary goal of SAR is prevention. By reporting suspicious activities, you help authorities act before a situation escalates into something more serious. It's about staying one step ahead and neutralizing potential threats early.

Statistics highlight the effectiveness of this approach. Data from the National SAR Initiative shows that timely reporting of suspicious activities led to a 20% reduction in crime rates in major cities[2]. This demonstrates the powerful impact of SAR on community safety. When suspicious activities are reported promptly, authorities can respond effectively, preventing crimes and enhancing overall security.

Privacy Considerations

It's crucial to remember that SAR is about behaviors, not personal characteristics. Reports should focus on what people are doing, not who they are. This means avoiding assumptions based on someone's appearance, race, or religion. SAR respects privacy by concentrating on actions that might indicate a potential threat.

When you report suspicious activity, ensure your observations are objective and behavior-focused. For instance, instead of describing someone by ethnicity, focus on what they are doing that seems suspicious. This approach ensures that SAR remains a tool for safety, not a means of discrimination.

Everyone's Role in SAR

While security officers play a significant role in SAR, everyone can participate. Whether you're a store employee, a commuter, or a

---

2. National SAR Initiative. (n.d.). *Timely reporting led to a 20% reduction in crime rates:* https://www.dhs.gov/national-sar-initiative

resident, your observations can contribute to community safety. The "See Something, Say Something" campaign emphasizes that everyone has a part to play.

Remember the quote, "Role of Security Officers: Security officers are crucial to the 'See Something, Say Something' campaign[3]. They're trained to understand what might be suspicious and know how to handle reports." As a security officer, your training and vigilance make you a key player in this initiative. But everyone's input is valuable.

In summary, SAR is a powerful tool for maintaining safety and preventing threats. Security officers and community members can contribute to a safer environment by understanding what it is and how to use it. Your role in observing and reporting suspicious activities is vital. Together, we can make a significant impact on community safety.

Role of Security Professionals in SAR

Security officers hold a pivotal position in the Suspicious Activity Reporting system. Their unique role often places them at the forefront of spotting potential risks and ensuring the community's safety. Here's how they contribute to SAR effectively:

---

3. Department of Homeland Security. (2016). *See Something, Say Something campaign: Role of security officers:* https://www.dhs.gov/see-something-say-something

Vigilance

Being a security officer requires constant vigilance. You need to be alert and watch for anything out of the ordinary. This vigilance is your first line of defense. It involves paying attention to details that others might overlook.

For instance, you might notice someone who seems out of place in a restricted area or acting nervously around a secure building. Your ability to spot these subtle signs can prevent potential threats. It's not just about looking; it's about seeing and understanding what might be a risk.

Assessing Situations

Once you've spotted something unusual, the next step is assessing the situation. Not every odd behavior is a threat, so it's crucial to determine the level of risk involved. This is where your training and experience come into play.

Imagine you see someone leaving a backpack in a hallway and walking away quickly. It could be harmless, but it could also be something more serious. Your job is to evaluate the context: Is the area known for high security? Does the person's behavior align with someone forgetting their bag, or does it seem more deliberate?

Your assessment should be swift but thorough. You're looking for cues and clues that help you determine whether the activity warrants further action. This ability to assess situations accurately ensures you respond appropriately without causing unnecessary alarm.

Gathering Information

When you identify suspicious activity, gathering detailed information is crucial. The more precise your report, the better the authorities can respond. This includes noting the time, location, descriptions of people involved, and precisely what they were doing.

For example, suppose you notice someone tampering with a security camera. In that case, you should document the location, the suspect's physical appearance, the exact time of the incident, and any other relevant details. This comprehensive information is vital for the next steps in the SAR process.

Reporting

Once you have gathered all the necessary details, the next step is to report the suspicious activity through the appropriate channels. This could be your own security team, law enforcement, or a designated reporting system. The key is to ensure the information reaches the right people quickly.

Remember, your report should be clear, concise, and focused on behaviors. Avoid making assumptions or including unnecessary details. Stick to the facts, and ensure your report is as accurate as possible.

Following Protocols

Every organization has specific protocols for handling suspicious activities. As a security officer, knowing and following these protocols is essential. This ensures that every report is dealt with correctly and efficiently.

For instance, your organization might have a procedure requiring immediate notification from higher authorities for certain types of threats. Following these protocols ensures the appropriate response is activated promptly, reducing the risk of mishandling a potential threat.

Post-Report Actions

After you've reported suspicious activity, you might need to take additional steps. These could involve monitoring the situation, assisting law enforcement, or implementing measures to ensure immediate safety.

Consider a scenario where you've reported a suspicious package. After the initial report, you need to secure the area, guide people to safety, or provide updates to the responding authorities. Your actions post-report are just as critical as the initial reporting, ensuring a comprehensive response to the threat.

Continuous Training and Improvement

Continuous training is essential to staying effective in SAR. This includes staying updated on new threats, learning from past incidents, and regularly reviewing SAR protocols.

A 2017 National Institute of Justice research paper demonstrated that security officers trained in SAR protocols are more effective in identifying and reporting potential threats[4]. This highlights the importance of ongoing education and training in maintaining high standards of vigilance and response.

Becoming the Eyes and Ears of Companies and the Community

Security officers are often described as the eyes and ears of the places they protect. This role goes beyond just watching; it's about being aware and connected to the surroundings, whether a company or a community. Here's why this role is so important:

Awareness

A big part of being the eyes and ears is staying aware. Security officers need to know what's normal for their area so they can spot when something isn't right. This means understanding the routines, the usual crowd, and the typical activities that happen day to day.

Think about your workplace. You know the regular employees, the usual visitors, and the standard routines. When something deviates from this norm, it catches your attention. This awareness is the foundation of effective SAR.

Connection to the Community

Security officers often interact with the same people regularly. This helps them build a connection with the community. When people know their security officer, they're more likely to report something suspicious or ask for help.

Consider a scenario where you've built a rapport with the local shop owners in your patrol area. They trust you and feel comfortable sharing concerns about suspicious activities. This connection enhances your effectiveness as a security officer, making you a trusted point of contact for the community.

Acting as a Deterrent

Security officers can prevent bad things from happening just by being present and alert. If someone is planning something dangerous or illegal, seeing a vigilant security officer might make them think twice.

Your visible presence is a powerful deterrent. It signals that the area is monitored and that any suspicious activity will be noticed and reported. This proactive approach can prevent incidents before they occur, contributing to a safer environment.

Quick Response

Because security officers are right there on the ground, they can respond quickly to situations. This can make a big difference in emergencies, whether helping someone hurt or stopping a dangerous situation from worsening.

Imagine you're on patrol, and you see someone collapse. Your immediate response to call for medical help and provide first aid can save a life. Your ability to act quickly and efficiently is critical to your role.

Sharing Information

Security officers often have valuable information about their areas. By sharing this with law enforcement or other security teams, they can help build a bigger picture of what's happening in the community. Remember, "Data from the National SAR Initiative shows that timely reporting of suspicious activities led to a 20% reduction in crime rates in major cities."

Your observations, when combined with those of others, create a comprehensive understanding of potential threats. This collaboration enhances the overall security strategy, making it more effective in preventing and responding to incidents.

Education and Training

Part of being the eyes and ears also means staying educated and trained. This could be learning about new security risks, practicing first aid, or understanding how to handle different kinds of emergencies.

Continuous learning ensures you're prepared for any situation. Whether it's a training session on the latest security technology or a refresher course on emergency procedures, staying informed and skilled is crucial for effective SAR.

See Something, Say Something' Campaign

The "See Something, Say Something" campaign is a national effort to encourage people to report suspicious activities. It's a simple idea, but it greatly impacts keeping everyone safe. Security officers play a key role in this campaign. Here's how it works and why it's important:

The Message

The campaign's main message is simple: if you see something that doesn't look right, you should say something about it. This could be an unattended bag, someone trying to open a locked door, or anything that seems out of place.

The power of this message lies in its simplicity. Everyone, regardless of their background or experience, can participate. It empowers individuals to take action and contribute to community safety.

Awareness

The campaign aims to make everyone more aware of their surroundings. By paying attention to what's happening around them, people can notice when something doesn't seem right.

Think about your daily routine. How often do you pay attention to your surroundings? The "See Something, Say Something" campaign encourages everyone to be more observant, turning passive bystanders into active participants in safety.

Encouraging Reports

Sometimes, people might see something suspicious but aren't sure if they should report it. The campaign encourages them to report anyway. It's better to report something that turns out to be harmless than to miss reporting something dangerous.

The statistics speak for themselves. "A 2016 U.S. Department of Homeland Security study found that public awareness campaigns like 'See Something, Say Something' increased reporting of suspicious activities by 40%." This shows that when people are encouraged to report, they do, leading to a safer community.

Role of Security Officers

Security officers are crucial to the "See Something, Say Something" campaign. They're trained to understand and know how to handle what might be suspicious reports. They can also help educate others about the importance of reporting. As a security officer, your expertise and vigilance are vital. You're not just a passive observer but an active community safety defender.

Building Trust

Part of the campaign is about building trust between the community and security forces. When people trust their security officers, they're more likely to report suspicious things.

Building trust involves being approachable, reliable, and professional. When community members see you as a trusted ally, they're more likely to share concerns and report suspicious activities, enhancing the campaign's overall effectiveness.

Response to Reports

When someone reports something, it must be appropriately handled. Security officers need to take every report seriously, investigate it, and then take the appropriate action based on what they find.

Your response to reports should be prompt and professional. Each report, regardless of how minor it might seem, deserves attention. Properly handling of these reports addresses potential threats and reinforces community trust in the reporting system.

Conclusion

As we conclude Chapter 3 on "Nationwide Suspicious Activity Reporting," it's clear that security officers' role in identifying and reporting suspicious activities is vital. From understanding Suspicious Activity Reporting to embracing their role as the eyes and ears of companies and communities, security officers are essential in keeping people safe.

The Importance of SAR

We learned that SAR is more than just a tool; it's a crucial part of national safety efforts. It helps stop dangerous situations before they start. By reporting suspicious activities, we contribute to a proactive approach to community safety.

Role of Security Professionals

Security officers aren't just guards; they're trained professionals who play a crucial role in spotting and reporting suspicious activities. Their judgment and quick action can make all the difference. Remember the study: "A 2017 research paper from the National Institute of Justice demonstrated that security officers trained in SAR protocols are more effective in identifying and reporting potential threats."

Being Vigilant

Security officers serve as the frontline observers of their environments. Their vigilance helps ensure the safety and security of the places they protect and those in them.

The Power of 'See Something, Say Something'

This campaign is a nationwide call to action. It emphasizes the importance of speaking up when something seems off. Security officers are pivotal in promoting this message and encouraging people to report.

Remember, as a security officer, your role is more than just monitoring; it's about actively keeping your environment safe. Your vigilance, ability to recognize and report suspicious activities, and commitment to the safety of your community make you an invaluable asset in the security field.

With this understanding, you're not just doing a job but

contributing to a larger effort to keep our communities safe. The responsibility is significant, but so is the impact of your work. Stay alert, stay informed, and remember: when you see something, say something. Together, we can make a significant difference in community safety.

Chapter Four

Report Writing

HAVE YOU EVER HAD to share a crucial moment with someone—perhaps a scenario you needed to explain to your boss in writing? That's precisely what report writing is for security officers, though the stakes are undeniably higher. For security officers, report writing isn't just a task; it's a cornerstone of your role. Why? Because a well-crafted report can safeguard communities, resolve conflicts, and even - determine court cases.

In this chapter, we will dive deep into report writing. Imagine you're not just filling out a form but crafting a narrative that has the power to inform and protect. We'll explore why report writing is so pivotal, the various types of reports you might compile, who will be reading your reports, and how to refine your writing to ensure clarity, precision, and - accuracy.

Writing a report might seem straightforward, but it's truly a skill—one that involves not just recounting facts but presenting them in a manner that is accessible and actionable for everyone who reads them. By the time we wrap up this chapter, you'll be equipped to write reports that aren't just professional but are clear, constructive, and crucial to your success as a security officer. This isn't just about becoming a better writer; it's about enhancing your effectiveness on the job and beyond.

"Writing a report is a big responsibility. It's not just about the facts; it's about making sure they are clear and useful to anyone who reads them[1]." This quote encapsulates what we aim for—reporting that transcends mere documentation to become vital to operational and legal success.

Why is this important? Consider this: The National Association of Security Professionals reports that clear and concise report writing can reduce the time spent on investigations by 30%[2]. Imagine the impact of that in an emergency or ongoing threat situation. Time saved could mean lives saved.

So, let's get started. Are you ready to master the art of report writing? Are you prepared to be responsible for documenting crucial details that could influence the course of an investigation or even the outcome of a legal proceeding? This chapter will provide you with the knowledge, tools, and examples to elevate your reporting

---

1. National Association of Security Professionals. (2019). *Writing a report is a big responsibility:* https://www.nasp.org/report-writing

2. National Association of Security Professionals. (2019). *Clear and concise report writing reduces investigation time by 30%:* https://www.nasp.org/statistics

skills to the level of your dedication and vigilance. Let's embark on this journey to becoming proficient security officers and exceptional communicators.

Purposes of a Report

When you sit down to write a report as a security officer, what do you think you're doing? Are you just filling out forms or playing a pivotal role in the security management ecosystem? Let's unpack this together and truly understand your report's multiple critical purposes.

Documenting Incidents

First and foremost, reports are historical records. Every time you document an incident—be it a theft, an accident, or any - particular activity—you create a record that captures that moment. This isn't just paperwork; it's a crucial tool for recalling and understanding events as they occur. Think about it: How often have you referred back to a previous incident to connect dots or inform your current understanding?

Legal Evidence

One of the most significant roles a report plays is in the legal arena. "A 2019 research article indicated that 90% of legal teams find well-written security reports crucial in court cases." Your report could be the critical piece of evidence that helps to clarify the sequence of events, proving what happened and potentially deciding the outcome of a court case. Every word you write could weigh heavily under the scrutiny of the law, making it imperative that your reports are clear, factual, and honest.

Communication Tool

Your reports also serve as a vital communication bridge. They inform your supervisors, colleagues, and sometimes even law enforcement agencies about what happened, shaping decisions and strategies. A well-drafted report can streamline responses and ensure everyone is on the same page, reducing misunderstandings and enhancing team efficiency.

Accountability

By documenting your actions and observations, - you are also demonstrating accountability. This shows that you are actively engaged in your duties, monitoring your environment, and taking responsibility for your area of control. It's a testament to your professionalism and commitment to safety.

Improving Security

Here's something to ponder: How can we improve if we don't learn from the past? Reports help organizations to analyze incidents and develop strategies to prevent future occurrences. Management can take proactive steps to strengthen safety measures by identifying patterns or repeated security breaches.

Training and Learning

Reports can be invaluable learning tools for new security officers. They provide real-life examples of situations that officers might face and offer insights into practical ways to handle them. A study published in the *International Journal of Security and Safety* demonstrated that comprehensive report-writing training improves the quality of incident documentation by 50%[3]. That's a substantial improvement, enhancing individual performance and the overall safety environment.

Refreshing Memory

If you've ever been in a situation where you had to recall details from months ago, you'll appreciate how a well-written report can refresh your memory. Especially in legal scenarios, where you might need to testify, having a detailed report can ensure that your testimony is accurate and reliable.

Each purpose underscores a fundamental truth: Report writing is not a mundane task but a critical security function. As you grasp the importance of each purpose, you begin to see that every report you write is a building block in the foundation of your career as a security officer. It's about more than just documenting; it's about making a significant impact.

---

3. International Journal of Security and Safety. (2019). *Comprehensive training improves report quality by 50%:* https://www.ijss.org/training

Are you ready to take this responsibility seriously? Are you prepared to use your reports not just as forms to be filled but as tools for communication, learning, and legal defense? Remember, every report you write enhances your role as a protector, a communicator, and a leader in the security field. Let's move on to understanding the different types of reports you might encounter and how each serves a unique function in your professional toolkit.

Types of Reports

In the diverse world of security work, report writing adapts to various needs and scenarios. Each type of report has a distinct purpose, shaping how you gather and present information. - Using these different reports is not just about knowing what to write but also about - understanding why and for whom you are writing. Let's explore some standard reports you might encounter as a security officer.

Incident Reports

Incident reports are perhaps the most common and pivotal among security reports. These are detailed accounts of specific incidents, such as thefts, assaults, or significant occurrences that disrupt normal operations. The precision and clarity of these reports can greatly influence the outcomes of investigations and legal proceedings. For example, documenting the sequence of events during a theft at a retail store not only aids in resolving the current incident but also helps develop preventive measures for the future.

Daily Activity Reports

As mundane as they might sound, daily activity reports are essential. They provide a log of what you did during your shift—areas patrolled, minor incidents noted, and general observations. These reports ensure continuity between shifts and maintain a routine check on regular operations, proving invaluable in environments where consistency and vigilance are key. Think of it as your daily diary, charting your stewardship of the space you're guarding.

Emergency Situation Reports

The emergency situation report comes into play in an emergency, such as a fire or medical crisis. This report details the nature of the emergency, the response initiated, and the outcomes of those actions. It's crucial to document the effectiveness of the response and review and improve emergency protocols. Writing these reports swiftly and succinctly can save lives and mitigate damages by ensuring that subsequent responders and management are well-informed and prepared for action.

Visitor Logs

Visitor logs are fundamental for facilities that require monitoring of entry and exit. These logs track who comes in and out, their purpose of visiting, and their duration of stay. This is vital for security in buildings with high visitor turnover and can be critical in emergency situations where knowing who is in the building could impact evacuation strategies and safety measures.

Maintenance Reports

A maintenance report is necessary when you notice something amiss, such as a faulty door lock or a broken surveillance camera. These reports are directed towards the facility management team to ensure that any potential security vulnerabilities are addressed swiftly. Effective maintenance reports are about listing defects and providing detailed, actionable information that can lead to quick resolutions. For instance, specifying the location, nature of the issue, and any temporary measures taken can significantly expedite the repair process.

Shift Handover Reports

Shift handover reports are crucial for ensuring seamless security coverage. These reports provide the incoming officer with an overview of what happened during the previous shift, including any ongoing situations or areas that require special attention. This continuous flow of information is vital for maintaining adequate security, as it ensures that no detail is lost in the transition between shifts. Imagine a scenario where an officer encounters suspicious activity near a restricted area during a night shift—this information must be passed on accurately and comprehensively to the next officer.

Each of these report types serves a specific function in the security management system, ensuring that information flows correctly and efficiently across all levels of the organization. Knowing how to write each report effectively ensures that you actively contribute to the security and well-being of the environment you are tasked to protect.

In security work, the quality of your reports directly impacts the response's effectiveness and the organization's overall security posture. Remember, your reports are often the first reference point in any security-related decision-making process. Therefore, mastering the different types of reports is not just about writing well—it's about ensuring that your writing leads to action and improvement.

As we delve deeper into the art of report writing, let's consider the audience of these reports. Understanding who reads your reports will further refine your ability to communicate effectively, ensuring your message is heard and acted upon. This brings us to our next crucial topic: Who are the readers of your reports, and how does knowing them shape how you write? Explore this in the next section to better tailor your reports to their needs.

Who Reads the Report You Write?

Understanding your audience is crucial in any communication, especially in security report writing. Your reports' clarity, detail, and tone can significantly impact how effectively your message is understood and acted upon. Let's explore who typically reads your reports and how this knowledge can shape your approach to writing them.

Security Management

Your immediate supervisors and the broader security management team are primary readers of your reports. They rely on your documentation to gauge security, make informed decisions, and strategize for future actions. For example, a detailed incident report can help management understand security breaches, leading to better-informed policy adjustments or training programs. The clearer and more comprehensive your reports, the better-equipped management is to uphold safety and improve security protocols.

Law Enforcement

Law enforcement officers may review your reports when incidents escalate or involve legal issues. These professionals look for clear, factual accounts to aid investigations or serve as evidence in legal proceedings. The accuracy of your reports can significantly impact the outcomes of legal cases or police investigations. For instance, a well-documented report of vandalism with precise times and suspect descriptions can streamline police efforts to apprehend and charge the perpetrators.

Legal Teams

In situations where security incidents lead to litigation, legal professionals might scrutinize your report. Lawyers and judges look for thorough and unbiased reports to build reliable narratives for court cases. As noted - in a 2019 research article, 90% of legal teams find well-written security reports crucial in court cases. This highlights the importance of maintaining a professional, objective, and meticulous standard in your report writing.

Company Executives

High-level executives within your company may also review your reports, primarily if the incidents significantly affect the business's operations or reputation. Executives need concise, clear reports that allow them to analyze quickly - the situation's impact and implications. For example, a report detailing recurrent security breaches in a company warehouse might prompt executives to allocate more resources to security infrastructure.

Other Staff

Depending on the incident and the organizational structure, other departmental staff, such as Human resources, operations, or facilities management, may access your reports. These readers often look for specific information relevant to their roles. For instance, a maintenance report detailing a faulty security gate would be crucial for the - facility team to prioritize repairs.

Insurance Companies

After incidents involving property damage or personal injury, insurance companies might review your reports to assess claims. These entities require detailed, factual narratives to process claims efficiently. Accurate descriptions of the incident, the extent of damage, and any preventive measures taken are crucial for timely claim resolution.

Knowing Your Audience

Each audience has specific expectations and needs from your reports. Here are some tailored tips for writing effectively for each reader:

- **For Management:** Focus on strategic insights, highlight patterns, and suggest improvements.

- **For Law Enforcement:** Provide detailed, factual descriptions and maintain a chronological order of events.

- **For Legal Teams:** Ensure accuracy and avoid subjective language to uphold objectivity.

- **For Executives:** Be concise and direct, highlighting the impact on business operations.

- **For Other Staff:** Include relevant operational details to assist in immediate actions or long-term planning.

- **For Insurance Companies:** Document factual and comprehensive details about incidents to support claims processing.

Understanding who reads your reports helps tailor the content and enhance the effectiveness of the communication. The better you understand your audience, the more effective your reports will be in achieving their purpose—whether it's securing a conviction, improving safety protocols, or informing strategic decisions.

As we move forward, let's delve into the building blocks of an excellent report. Knowing the fundamentals of crafting your report will ensure that it meets the high standards expected by all these diverse readers, providing them with the information they need to act decisively and appropriately.

The Building Blocks of Report Writing

Writing a good security report is akin to constructing a building; every element, from the foundation to the roof, plays a crucial role in ensuring its integrity. Just as a vital building stands firm against challenges, a well-constructed report provides a reliable, clear, and effective account of events that can withstand scrutiny and facilitate action. Let's break down the essential components of effective report writing in security.

Who

Identifying all involved parties accurately is vital. This includes suspects, victims, and witnesses. Detailing the 'Who' in your report requires precision:

- **Suspects:** Describe with as much detail as possible. Include physical appearance, clothing, behaviors, and any distinguishing features. Each suspect should be distinctly described to avoid confusion.

- **Victims:** Document their identities, conditions during the incident, and interactions with them.

- **Witnesses:** Include their contact information and a

summary of their statements. Witnesses can provide pivotal corroborative details or contrasting accounts that may affect the investigation.

What

Describing 'What' happened is the core of your report. Include the specific nature of the incident - such as specific actions taken by the perpetrators, any property damaged or stolen, and the response by security personnel. Be factual and avoid subjective interpretations; stick to observable facts and verifiable information.

Where

The 'Where' provides context and aids in understanding the incident's environment. Be specific about locations: give exact addresses, describe the area within a building, and mention any relevant environmental factors. Accurate location details are essential for effective response and future preventive measures.

When

Timing can be critical in security work. Document the date and exact time of the incident and, if relevant, its duration. Precise timing can help verify alibis, understand the sequence of events, and coordinate responses.

Why

Although you may not always know the motives behind an incident, it's essential to include any - known reasons. Information from witnesses or previous incidents might provide insight into the 'Why.' This can help understand threats and prevent future incidents.

How

Detail how the incident unfolded and the - actions taken. This should include how the security team managed the situation, interactions with law enforcement, and any immediate measures implemented to control the situation or mitigate damage.

Interaction with Law Enforcement and Emergency Responders

Include detailed accounts of interactions with law enforcement and emergency services. Note the times of their arrival, the information shared, actions taken, and how they contributed to resolving the incident. This information is crucial for a comprehensive understanding of the response and reviewing security operations' efficiency.

Writing Tips

To make your report effective, keep these writing tips in mind:

- **Clarity:** Use simple, direct language. Avoid jargon or overly technical terms unless necessary, and use only commonly recognizable abbreviations.

- **Accuracy:** Ensure all information is correct. Double-check dates, names, descriptions, and other factual information.

- **Objectivity:** Maintain a neutral tone. Report the facts without letting personal feelings or assumptions influence the content.

- **Detail:** Include all necessary details but avoid irrelevant information that does not contribute to a clear understanding of the incident.

- **Conciseness:** Be as concise as possible while providing complete information. Every sentence should serve a purpose.

- **Organization:** Structure your report logically. Use headings and subheadings to guide the reader through the content.

- **Proofreading:** Always review your report for errors. Spelling, grammar, and punctuation mistakes can undermine the professionalism of your writing.

- **Consistency:** Use a consistent format throughout your report. This includes time formats, terminologies, and descriptions.

Mastering these building blocks will elevate your report writing skills, making your reports more professional and more effective in communicating crucial information. These elements will become second nature with practice, enhancing your ability to document and report security incidents accurately and efficiently.

Next, we will tackle the common pitfalls in report writing and how to avoid them, ensuring your reports remain clear, professional, and impactful.

Common Problems in Report Writing

Even the most seasoned security officers can encounter challenges in report writing. Recognizing these common issues and understanding how to avoid them is crucial for maintaining the quality and effectiveness of your reports. Here's a guide to identifying and overcoming the typical problems that compromise your report writing.

Vagueness

A vague report can leave too much room for interpretation, potentially leading to embarrassing cross-examinations during trials, misunderstandings, or incorrect conclusions. To combat vagueness:

- **Be Specific:** Instead of writing "a large number of items were stolen," specify exactly how many items were taken—detailed descriptions, actions, and responses as precisely as possible.

- **Use Concrete Details:** Describe people, places, and actions clearly. For example, instead of saying, "The suspect was tall," note the estimated height.

Bias

Objectivity is key in security reporting. Personal biases should not influence the content of your reports.

- **Stick to Facts:** Focus on what you observed directly, not your opinions or feelings about those observations.

- **Equal Treatment:** Ensure that all individuals involved are described with the same level of detail and neutrality.

Grammatical Errors

Poor grammar can undermine the professionalism of your report and distract from its content.

- **Reviews:** Review your reports to help identify and correct mistakes.

- **Read Aloud:** Reading your report out loud can help you catch errors you might miss when reading silently.

Too Much Information

Overloading a report with unnecessary details can make it difficult to discern the key points.

- **Stay Relevant:** Include only information directly related to the incident and its outcomes.

- **Prioritize Information:** Start with the most critical details and additional context or background information as needed.

Repetition

Repeating information can be redundant and make your report longer without adding value.

- **Consolidate Information:** If the same information applies to multiple sections of the report, mention it once and refer back to it as needed.

- **Review for Redundancy:** Ensure each piece of information in your report adds something new to the reader's understanding.

Passive Voice

Using passive voice can make reports less direct and harder to follow.

- **Use Active Voice:** Active voice makes your writing clearer and more assertive. For example, instead of saying, "The officer locked the door," say, "The officer locked the door."

Informal Language

Maintaining a professional tone is essential in report writing.

- **Avoid Slang and Colloquialisms:** Use formal language appropriate for a professional document.

- **Professional Tone:** Keep the tone serious and focused, suitable for the gravity of security work.

Addressing these common issues can enhance the clarity, accuracy, and professionalism of your reports. Each report you write not only records your daily responsibilities but also reflects your competence and reliability as a security officer.

Reviewing Your Report

Before submitting your report, it's crucial to thoroughly review it to ensure it meets all necessary standards and effectively communicates the required information. Here's how to conduct a final review of your report:

Check for Accuracy

Make sure all factual information is correct. Verify dates, times, names, and descriptions for accuracy. Errors in these details can compromise the credibility of your report and potentially impact investigations or legal outcomes.

Ensure Completeness

Review your report to ensure it includes all relevant information to understand the incident fully. Ensure you've addressed the situation's 'Who, What, When, Where, Why, and How'.

Proofread

Check for spelling, grammar, and punctuation errors. These mistakes can distract readers and detract from the professionalism of your report.

Get Feedback

Have a colleague or supervisor review your report. A second pair of eyes can catch errors you might have missed and provide feedback that can improve the quality of your report.

Make Revisions

Based on your review and feedback received, make necessary revisions to your report. Adjustments include clarifying ambiguous sections, adding missing details, or correcting factual inaccuracies.

Reviewing your report is the final step in ensuring it serves its purpose effectively—documenting an incident, informing future actions, or providing evidence in legal cases. This step demonstrates your commitment to professionalism and attention to detail, essential for a successful career in security.

By following these steps, you ensure that each report you write meets the required standards and contributes positively to your professional role and the broader goals of your security team.

Conclusion

Throughout this chapter, we have thoroughly explored the multifaceted skill of report writing in the security profession. From understanding the various purposes and types of reports to pinpointing who reads these reports and how to communicate the right information effectively, we've covered the essential landscape of what makes effective report writing so crucial in security work.

We've delved into the fundamental components of a strong report—clarity, accuracy, objectivity, and conciseness—and discussed the common pitfalls that can undermine these qualities. We've also provided practical advice on avoiding these issues, ensuring that every report you write is professional and impactful.

The role of a security officer involves much more than just maintaining order; it requires being a diligent observer, a precise communicator, and a reliable recorder of events. Each report you write is a testament to your role as a key player in the security landscape, influencing operational strategies, legal outcomes, and public safety.

Let's reflect on a few key takeaways:

- **The importance of clarity and detail** must be balanced. Your reports must be easy to understand and free of ambiguity to effectively guide others' decisions and actions.

- **Accuracy and objectivity** are your allies in establishing trust and credibility, not only with your immediate supervisors but also with external entities like law enforcement and the judicial system.

- **Understanding your audience** and tailoring your reports to meet their specific needs can significantly enhance the effectiveness of the information you provide.

- **Reviewing your work** is essential. This step ensures that your reports are free from errors and omissions and reflect your professionalism and dedication to your role.

As you progress in your security career, remember that report writing is a powerful tool. It's not just about documenting what happened; it's about telling a story that can prevent future incidents, guide strategic decisions, and sometimes even shape legal landscapes.

Your ability to write detailed, clear, and actionable reports will set you apart as a professional in your field. Embrace this skill, refine it, and use it to contribute to the safety and security of your environment. Each report you write not only narrates an incident but also weaves the larger story of your commitment to upholding safety, ensuring justice, and enhancing your organization's security measures.

In conclusion, remember that excellence in report writing is only achieved after some time. It requires practice, attention to detail, and a proactive approach to continuous improvement. As you hone this skill, you contribute to your professional growth and the broader mission of creating a secure, orderly, and safe environment. Keep striving to enhance your reporting skills, and you'll find that your efforts greatly enrich your capabilities and the effectiveness of your role as a security officer.

Chapter Five
Managing Bomb Threats

I MAGINE YOU'RE AT YOUR post, and suddenly, the reality of a bomb threat looms. The weight of the moment falls on your shoulders—as a security officer, the decisions you make next are critical. It's a severe risk, not just to the safety of the people and property you protect but also to your safety. This isn't just about following protocol; it's about leadership in moments of crisis.

This chapter will guide you through managing bomb threats effectively, with a focus on understanding, preparation, and decisive action. Why do we focus so intensely on these threats? Because in 2019, the FBI reported over 1,000 bomb threats across the United States[1]. This stark number underlines the critical need for security personnel to be adept in handling such high-stakes situations.

We will explore the key components of bomb threat management: from the initial reception of a threat through the coordination of an

---

1. FBI. (2019). *Effective bomb threat response begins with preparation:* https://www.fbi.gov/resources

effective response to the reflective process that follows every incident. Each phase is an opportunity to demonstrate competence and calm under pressure, ensuring safety and mitigating risk.

"Effective response to bomb threats begins with thorough preparation. Knowing the layout of the facilities, establishing clear communication channels, and having well-practiced evacuation plans are essential." This advice isn't just procedural; it's foundational to the confidence and quick action required in these scenarios. How well do you know your environment? How quickly can you communicate a threat? The answers to these questions can mean the difference between chaos and order, harm and safety.

Security officers must be equipped not just with the knowledge of what to do but with the critical thinking skills necessary to evaluate the seriousness of a situation and make informed decisions swiftly. The responsibility is immense, but so is the opportunity to prevent harm and safeguard lives.

As we progress through this chapter, remember that each bomb threat, whether a false alarm or a genuine crisis, offers a chance for reflection and learning. "Every bomb threat is an opportunity to assess the strength of your response and refine your strategies, ensuring you're better prepared for any challenge.

Stay engaged as we unpack the complexities of bomb threat management, enhancing your readiness to face potential dangers with a strategic and composed mindset. Are you ready to step into this critical role? Let's bolster your understanding and equip you with the tools you need to handle these threats with expertise and assurance.

Understanding Common Methods of Making Bomb Threats

Regarding bomb threats, the delivery method can tell you a lot about the level of urgency and the type of response required. Understanding these methods is not just about reacting correctly—it's about anticipating, preparing, and neutralizing threats before they escalate. Let's explore the common channels through which these threats are communicated, equipping you with the knowledge to effectively identify and assess potential dangers.

1. Telephone Calls

Imagine this: a phone rings, and on the other end, a voice claims there's a bomb in the building. Telephone threats are direct and often aim to instill immediate panic. The caller might provide specific details or make demands. Here's what you do:

- **Stay calm** and keep the caller engaged. The longer they talk, the more information you can gather.

- **Record details**: Note the caller's voice, any background noises, and the specific words used.

- **Ask direct questions**: If possible, inquire about the bomb's location, the time set for detonation, and reasons for the threat.

This method requires quick thinking and precise communication. Training for such scenarios can significantly enhance response times and decision-making accuracy—a study found that regular drills considerably boost these skills among security personnel.

2. Email and Electronic Messages

Digital threats come with their own set of challenges. An email or electronic message can be sent anonymously and distributed widely with just a few clicks. Here's your action plan:

- **Preserve the evidence**: Save copies of the messages, including headers and metadata.

- **Assess the content**: Look for specifics that might indicate the authenticity of the threat.

- **Report immediately**: Inform your superiors and relevant authorities; digital forensics might be needed to trace the source.

Remember, "Less than 10% of bomb threats result in the discovery of an actual explosive device, but each threat must be treated with utmost seriousness to ensure safety[2]."

---

2. Security Industry Reports. (2019). *Less than 10% of bomb threats result in the discovery of an explosive device*: https://www.securityindustry.org/research

3. Social Media Platforms

Social media amplifies the reach of bomb threats, potentially causing widespread panic. Monitoring these platforms requires diligence and a proactive strategy.

- **Monitor effectively**: Use tools to track mentions of your organization and related threats.

- **Collaborate with platforms**: Work with social media companies to trace the origin of the threat and shut down harmful posts.

- **Communicate clearly**: Informing the public about the situation and your response can help mitigate panic and misinformation.

4. Written Notes or Letters

Old-school tactics like written threats still exist. They can provide physical clues that are invaluable in an investigation.

- **Handle with care**: Preserve fingerprints or DNA that may be on the document.

- **Analyze the handwriting and materials**: These can offer clues about the sender.

- **Document everything**: Keep records of how and when the letter was found and by whom.

5. Symbolic or Indirect Threats

Sometimes, the threat is more subtle—like an unattended package left in a strategic location. These situations require a sharp eye and a cautious approach.

- **Evaluate the surroundings**: Understand why a particular location might be chosen for leaving a suspicious package.

- **Use your training**: Respond according to your organization's protocols for suspicious packages.

Every method discussed here presents unique challenges, but a comprehensive understanding and prepared approach can make all the difference. The FBI's report of over 1,000 bomb threats in 2019 underscores the critical nature of being prepared for these scenarios[3].

"A study on the effectiveness of bomb threat response protocols found that regular training and drills significantly enhance response times and decision-making accuracy among security personnel[4]." Utilizing this insight, ensure your team knows these common methods and practices them in quick and effective responses.

As we transition to pre-planning strategies in the next section,

---

3. FBI. (2019). *Over 1,000 bomb threats reported in the U.S.*: https://www.fbi.gov/statistics

4. National Institute of Justice. (2018). *Effectiveness of bomb threat response protocols*: https://www.nij.ojp.gov/research

reflect on this: How well-prepared are you to handle a bomb threat communicated through these different channels? Are your current training and response strategies comprehensive enough to cover these scenarios?

Pre-Planning

"Effective response to bomb threats begins with thorough preparation." This isn't just a saying; it's a cornerstone of security work. In bomb threat scenarios, the groundwork you lay before a threat ever materializes is what truly empowers you to manage and mitigate risks effectively. Let's explore the essential components of pre-planning that every security officer needs to master.

Understanding the Facility

Know your terrain. Whether you're guarding a skyscraper, a school, or a shopping center, intimate knowledge of the layout is your first line of defense. Familiarize yourself with:

- **All exits and entry points**: Quick evacuation and access control depend on it.

- **Critical areas**: Where are the high-risk spots? These are areas like utility rooms, major halls, and public gathering spaces.

- **Surveillance blind spots**: Where are your cameras not reaching? Identifying these can help in placing temporary cameras or assigning patrol routes.

Having a detailed facility map accessible to all security team members can save precious minutes during a crisis. Regular walk-throughs and drills in different areas keep your familiarity with the venue fresh.

Establishing Communication Channels

Clear and swift communication can make the difference between chaos and order. Establish dedicated lines for:

- **Internal communication**: Ensure all security personnel can communicate instantly with each other and the control room.

- **External communication**: Maintain updated contacts for local law enforcement, bomb squads, and emergency services. Know who to call, when to call, and what information to relay without hesitation.

Implementing a standardized communication protocol, including the use of code words for discreet yet clear communication during emergencies, ensures everyone on your team knows how to report and respond.

Evacuation Plans

"Knowing the layout of the facility, establishing clear communication channels, and having well-practiced evacuation plans are essential." This includes:

- **Clearly marked evacuation routes**: These should be posted throughout the facility and included in training sessions.

- **Designated safe areas**: Know where to direct evacuees away from potential threats.

- **Regular drills**: Conduct these drills at varying times and under different scenarios to ensure staff and occupants are familiar with procedures.

The effectiveness of evacuation plans is not just in their creation but in their implementation and regular practice.

Threat Assessment Protocols

Developing a methodical approach to assessing the credibility of a threat saves time and directs resources appropriately. This involves:

- **Criteria for assessing threats**: Establish clear guidelines for what constitutes a credible threat.

- **Decision-making process**: Who makes the assessment? How quickly do they need to decide? What actions should follow an assessment?

Training on these protocols ensures that every officer is prepared to make quick and informed decisions under pressure.

Training and Education

"A study on the effectiveness of bomb threat response protocols found that regular training and drills significantly enhance response times and decision-making accuracy among security personnel." Continual training is crucial. It should cover:

- **Scenario-based drills**: These help security personnel experience simulated threats in a controlled environment, building their confidence and honing their skills.

- **Latest techniques and technologies**: Modern security preparedness requires keeping abreast of new security technologies and evolving threat tactics.

Equipment Readiness

Lastly, ensure all necessary equipment is available and in good working order. This includes:

- **Bomb detection devices**: Regularly check and maintain them.

- **Communication tools**: Test radios and other communication devices frequently.

- **First aid kits and emergency supplies**: Keep them stocked and accessible.

In summary, pre-planning is about being prepared for the worst while striving for the best. Each element of your preparation plays a pivotal role in the overall effectiveness of your response to bomb threats. The more thorough your preparation, the more confident and effective your response will be.

As we detail the specific roles and responsibilities during a bomb threat in the next section, remember this: preparation is the bedrock upon which successful incident management is built. Are you ready to explore how each team member contributes to managing a bomb threat effectively? Let's continue to build on this foundation and ensure that when a threat occurs, your team is not just reacting; they are taking control.

Bomb Management Personnel

In managing bomb threats, the composition and readiness of your personnel are as critical as any plan or procedure. Effective response hinges on individual capabilities and how well each member understands and executes their role within a coordinated effort. Let's dissect the roles and responsibilities of each critical team member involved in bomb threat management, equipping you to ensure that every link in this chain is strong and effective.

Security Officers

At the frontline are the security officers—the eyes and ears on the ground. In the event of a bomb threat, their roles include:

- **Initial Assessment**: They are often the first to receive reports of threats or to identify suspicious items. Quick, accurate assessment and communication of the situation are crucial.

- **Evacuation Management**: They direct and manage the evacuation of the premises, ensuring that all occupants proceed to designated safe areas calmly and efficiently.

- **Perimeter Security**: After evacuation, securing the perimeter to prevent unauthorized access or suspects' potential escape is vital.

Security officers must maintain a high level of vigilance and readiness. Regular threat detection and response training is essential to ensure they are prepared to act decisively and wisely.

Bomb Squad

When a potential bomb is identified, the bomb squad is called in. These specialists are highly trained in handling explosive devices and suspicious packages. Their responsibilities include:

- **Assessment and Neutralization**: They assess and, if necessary, neutralize the device using specialized equipment and techniques.

- **Evidence Collection**: Post-incident, the bomb squad collects evidence that can aid in criminal investigations.

- **Advisory Role**: They provide expert advice and guidance to security teams and decision-makers during the threat.

Collaboration between security officers and bomb squads must be seamless; clear communication and trust are imperative for the safety and effectiveness of both teams.

Emergency Services

Emergency responders encompass paramedics, firefighters, and other emergency services. Their readiness to respond quickly and effectively can be a matter of life and death. They are responsible for:

- **Medical Aid**: Providing immediate medical attention to injured persons during and after an evacuation.

- **Fire Safety**: Addressing any fire hazards that might arise from an explosive device or from evacuation processes.

- **Support in Evacuation**: This involves assisting in the safe and orderly evacuation of people, particularly those with disabilities or injuries.

Training with emergency services on integrated response plans ensures that all teams are synchronized and that each knows their role in the broader emergency response.

Facility Management

Facility managers provide critical infrastructure information that can assist in the search and neutralization of threats. Their responsibilities include:

- **Facility Layout Information**: Provide detailed maps and blueprints of the building, which are crucial for evacuation and searching procedures.

- **Infrastructure Control**: Managing essential systems like

HVAC, which might need to be shut down to prevent the spread of potential toxins from a bomb.

- **Post-Incident Recovery**: Facilitating the return to normal operations once the threat is neutralized.

Communication and Control Center Personnel

These individuals coordinate the bomb threat response by managing communications across all teams and with external agencies. They ensure:

- **Information Flow**: Critical information is relayed promptly and accurately to all relevant parties.

- **Resource Allocation**: Resources are directed where needed most, ensuring efficient use of personnel and equipment.

- **Record Keeping**: All communications and decisions are logged for post-incident analysis and for legal accountability.

The communication center acts as the hub of information and command, keeping the response efforts unified and directed.

Administrative Staff

Often overlooked, administrative personnel play vital roles, especially in larger facilities. They handle:

- **Notification**: Informing staff and visitors about the threat and evacuation procedures.

- **Liaison**: Acting as a point of contact for families, the media, and other external parties.

- **Documentation**: Maintaining records of the incident for insurance, legal, and historical purposes.

Each member of this comprehensive team plays a vital role in managing bomb threats. As we move forward, remember: "Every bomb threat, whether a false" or a genuine crisis, offers an opportunity for reflection and learning." Post-incident reviews and debriefings are crucial for evaluating the response's effectiveness and improving future preparedness.

The roles are defined, and the responsibilities are clear. But what drives someone to make a bomb threat? Understanding the motivations behind these threats is critical for assessing the danger and preventing future incidents. Let's explore the reasons behind bomb threats and how this knowledge can inform and refine your security strategies.

Reasons for Bomb Threats

Understanding the motivations behind bomb threats is crucial for security officers. Knowing why someone might issue such a threat helps assess the threat's credibility and devise effective responses. Let's explore the common motivations behind bomb threats and how understanding these can enhance your security strategies.

Criminal Intent

Often, bomb threats are used as a tool to facilitate other criminal activities. For instance, a thief might call in a bomb threat to divert law enforcement's attention away from a robbery happening elsewhere. In other cases, the threat itself could be an attempt at extortion. Recognizing this, security officers need to be vigilant about:

- **Concurrent Activities**: Whenever a bomb threat is reported, be aware of other activities that might be happening simultaneously. Are there any unusual movements or activities in different parts of the facility?

- **Patterns of Behavior**: Over time, you might notice patterns in the timing and location of threats. This information can be critical in anticipating and preventing criminal actions.

Political or Ideological Reasons

Some threats are motivated by political agendas or ideological beliefs. Terrorist groups or individuals might use bomb threats to spread fear, disrupt daily life, or draw attention to their cause. Demands or statements often accompany these threats:

- **Assessing Credibility**: Political or ideological threats might include specific details or demands. Analyze these to assess the threat's seriousness.

- **Cooperation with Authorities**: Engage with law enforcement and counter-terrorism units. They have the expertise and resources to handle politically motivated threats.

Personal Vendettas

Personal grudges or revenge can also motivate individuals to make bomb threats. This is often seen in workplace disputes, disgruntled former employees, or conflicts within the community:

- **Knowing Your Environment**: Be aware of any ongoing disputes or issues within your facility that could escalate to this level.

- **Discreet Monitoring**: Use surveillance and monitoring to identify potential threats early on. Look for signs of agitation or unusual behavior among employees or visitors.

Mental Health Issues

Mental health issues can lead individuals to issue bomb threats as a cry for help or as an expression of distress. These threats can be particularly challenging to assess because they might not follow the usual patterns of criminal or ideological threats:

- **Training on Mental Health**: Security personnel should receive training on recognizing signs of mental distress and how to respond compassionately yet firmly.

- **Coordination with Mental Health Professionals**: Work with mental health professionals to assess and address the situation, ensuring the safety of all involved.

Pranks or Hoaxes

Unfortunately, bomb threats are sometimes made as pranks, particularly in school or college environments. While these may not be serious, they must always be treated with caution:

- **Educational Programs**: Implement programs to educate students and staff about the seriousness of bomb threats and the consequences of making such threats.

- **Consistent Response**: Always respond to threats with the same level of seriousness, even if they seem to be pranks, to maintain a culture of safety and preparedness.

Attention Seeking

Some individuals make bomb threats to seek attention or feel powerful. These threats might lack the specificity or follow-through of more serious threats but can still cause significant disruption:

- **Profile the Behavior**: Look for patterns in the behavior of attention-seeking individuals. They might escalate from smaller disturbances to more serious threats.

- **Intervention Strategies**: Develop intervention strategies to address the underlying needs for attention or validation in a way that discourages harmful behaviors.

Understanding these motivations helps in tailoring your response strategies. For instance, recognizing a threat as part of a larger criminal plot allows you to coordinate more effectively with law enforcement. The key takeaway here is that every bomb threat, regardless of its source, must be treated with utmost seriousness. "Less than 10% of bomb threats result in the discovery of an actual explosive device, but each threat must be treated with utmost seriousness to ensure safety." Your role as a security officer involves responding to these threats and understanding the factors that contribute to them.

As we proceed to the next section, we'll evaluate these threats and make critical decisions under pressure. How do you assess a threat's credibility? What are the steps for making informed decisions quickly and effectively?

Evaluating the Threat and Making Decisions

When faced with a bomb threat, the ability to swiftly and accurately evaluate the situation is paramount. This section delves into the processes and critical thinking skills needed to assess the credibility of a threat and make informed decisions. The steps outlined here will equip you to handle such high-pressure scenarios with confidence and precision.

Initial Assessment

The first moment after receiving a bomb threat is crucial. You must gather as much information as possible to make an informed decision. Consider the following:

- **Details of the Threat**: Analyze the specificity of the details provided. Are there exact times, locations, and descriptions of the bomb?

- **Context and Credibility**: Consider the context of the threat. Is there any known history of threats or incidents at the location? Is the threat consistent with known patterns of behavior for the type of establishment you are protecting?

Information Gathering

Quickly gather information to evaluate the seriousness of the threat:

- **Engage with the Source**: If the threat is made via telephone, keep the caller engaged. Ask specific questions about the bomb's location, the type of device, and the reasons for the threat. Note the caller's voice, background noises, and language used.

- **Collect Evidence**: For threats made through written notes, emails, or social media, preserve all physical and digital evidence. This includes saving emails, taking screenshots, and securing any physical documents for forensic analysis.

Consulting with Experts

Involving experts can significantly enhance your threat assessment process:

- **Law Enforcement and Bomb Squads**: Contact these authorities immediately. Their expertise is invaluable in determining the credibility of the threat and deciding on the next steps.

- **Emergency Services**: Engage with medical and fire services early on to ensure they are on standby and ready to respond if needed.

Decision to Evacuate

One of the most critical decisions is whether to evacuate the building or area. The decision to evacuate should be made by a designated person based on company policy in managing bomb threats. This decision should be based on:

- **Threat Credibility**: Weigh the details and context of the threat. If the threat seems credible, err on the side of caution.

- **Risk to Life and Property**: Consider the potential impact of the bomb. If the potential damage is high, even a low-credibility threat might warrant evacuation.

- **Evacuation Protocols**: Follow established evacuation procedures to ensure order and efficiency. Ensure that all personnel and visitors are aware of the evacuation routes and assembly points.

Communication Strategy

Clear, concise communication is essential to managing a bomb threat effectively:

- **Internal Communication**: Inform all relevant personnel about the threat and the actions being taken. Use established protocols to ensure everyone receives the same information promptly.

- **External Communication**: Notify law enforcement, emergency services, and, if necessary, the public. Ensure that the information shared is accurate and helps to prevent panic.

Post-Threat Evaluation

After the threat has been addressed, it's crucial to conduct a thorough evaluation of the response:

- **Debriefing Sessions**: Hold debriefing sessions with all involved personnel to review the incident. Identify what went well and where shortcomings existed.

- **Incident Report**: Document the entire incident, including the initial threat, the response actions taken, and the outcomes. This report is invaluable for future training and improving response protocols.

Reflect and Improve

"Every bomb threat, whether a false alarm or a genuine crisis, offers an opportunity for reflection and learning." Use each incident as a chance to refine your strategies:

- **Strengths and Weaknesses**: Identify the strengths in your response and areas that need improvement.

- **Refine Protocols**: Adjust your threat assessment and response protocols based on the lessons learned.

- **Continuous Training**: Implement additional training sessions to address any identified gaps in knowledge or practice.

Case Study: Evaluating a Real Threat

Consider this scenario: A large shopping mall receives a bomb threat via telephone. The caller provides specific details about the bomb's location and the timing of its detonation. The security team immediately engages the caller to gather more information while simultaneously notifying law enforcement. As the details unfold, it becomes clear that the threat is credible, and an evacuation is ordered.

During the evacuation, the communication center coordinates with emergency services, ensuring that medical teams are on standby. The bomb squad arrives, assesses the situation, and successfully neutralizes the threat. Post-incident, the security team holds a debriefing session to review the response, leading to refinements in their evacuation protocols and threat assessment procedures.

Evaluating a bomb threat and making critical decisions requires a combination of quick thinking, detailed protocols, and effective communication. Understanding the factors involved and using the tools at your disposal allows you to navigate these high-pressure situations effectively.

As we move on to the next section, we will explore the differences between unattended and suspicious packages. Remember that every decision you make in these moments can have far-reaching implications. Your ability to evaluate and act swiftly and accurately is crucial.

Unattended vs. Suspicious Package Response

In bomb threat management, distinguishing between unattended and suspicious packages is crucial for ensuring safety and preventing unnecessary panic. As a security officer, your ability to evaluate and respond appropriately to these scenarios can significantly impact your environment's overall security and order.

Unattended Packages

Unattended packages are items that seem out of place but do not exhibit overt signs of danger. These might include forgotten bags, misplaced boxes, or other items left in public areas. Here's how to approach them:

1. **Initial Assessment**

- **Location and Context**: Evaluate where the package is located. Is it in a high-traffic area where someone might have inadvertently left it, or in a secluded spot where it seems more suspicious?

- **Duration**: Consider how long the package has been there. Items left for a short period might simply be misplaced, while those left for longer could be more concerning.

2. **Caution and Observation**

   - **Visual Inspection**: Without touching the package, visually inspect it for any unusual characteristics. Look for wires, unusual shapes, or signs of tampering.

   - **Inquire Locally**: Ask nearby people if they know anything about the package. Often, unattended items belong to someone nearby who simply forgot them.

3. **Follow Protocol**

   - **Report**: If the package remains unclaimed and its nature is unclear, follow your organization's protocol. This typically involves alerting a supervisor or calling law enforcement for further assessment.

   - **Evacuate if Necessary**: If there are any signs of potential danger, initiate evacuation procedures as a precautionary measure.

Suspicious Packages

Suspicious packages exhibit characteristics that raise immediate concern and require a more urgent response. These items often display specific warning signs that indicate a potential threat.

1. **Immediate Red Flags**

    - **Visual Indicators**: Look for wires, batteries, excessive tape, or strange odors emanating from the package. These are all classic signs of a potentially dangerous item.

    - **Location**: Packages placed in hidden or strategic locations, such as near entry points of critical infrastructure, should be treated with heightened suspicion.

2. **Do Not Touch**

    - **Maintain Distance**: Never touch, move, or disturb a suspicious package. Handling the package could trigger an explosive device.

    - **Establish a Perimeter**: Set up a safe perimeter around the package. The size of the perimeter should be based on the suspected severity of the threat, usually extending far beyond the immediate vicinity of the package.

1. **Notify Authorities**

    - **Call Law Enforcement**: Contact local authorities, including the bomb squad. Provide them with detailed information about the package's appearance, location, and any observations you have made.

    - **Use Communication Protocols**: Ensure clear and precise communication with all involved parties to avoid misinformation and unnecessary panic.

2. **Document Observations**

    - **Record Details**: Document your observations while maintaining a safe distance. Note the time the package was found, its appearance, and other relevant details. This information is crucial for law enforcement and bomb disposal experts.

Practical Examples

Unattended Package Example: Imagine you're patrolling a busy shopping mall and notice a backpack left on a bench. You inquire with nearby shoppers, but no one claims it. Upon visual inspection, you see nothing unusual—no wires, no suspicious markings. You follow protocol, reporting the unattended bag to your supervisor and local law enforcement, who then handle it according to procedures. The owner is eventually found, having simply forgotten the bag.

Suspicious Package Example: Consider a different scenario where you find a small box tucked under a stairwell in an office building. The box is taped excessively, with wires protruding. Recognizing the danger, you immediately set up a perimeter, ensuring no one approaches the area. Following your company policy in managing bomb threats, you should notify your supervisor and law enforcement, providing them with all necessary details. When law enforcement arrives, they will assess the package and safely neutralize the threat.

Commonalities in Response

Despite the differences between unattended and suspicious packages, several key principles apply to both scenarios:

- **Safety First**: The primary goal is always to ensure the safety of people in the vicinity. Never take unnecessary risks.

- **Clear Communication**: Maintain clear lines of communication with your team, law enforcement, and emergency services to ensure everyone is informed and coordinated.

- **Avoid Panic**: Handle the situation calmly and professionally to avoid creating panic among staff and the public.

Reflection and Continuous Improvement

Every incident involving an unattended or suspicious package offers an opportunity for learning and improvement. After each event, conduct a debrief to review the response:

- **What Went Well?**: Identify the strengths in your response strategy.

- **Areas for Improvement**: Determine what could have been done better and update your protocols accordingly.

- **Training Needs**: Implement additional training or drills based on lessons learned to ensure continuous improvement in your response capabilities.

Handling unattended and suspicious packages effectively requires a blend of caution, quick thinking, and adherence to established protocols. By distinguishing between these two types of packages and responding appropriately, you can significantly enhance the safety and security of your environment.

As we move to the next section on search techniques, consider this: Are your current procedures for dealing with packages robust and well-practiced? Do you and your team feel confident in identifying and responding to potential threats? Let's build on this foundation and explore the search techniques that further bolster your capabilities in managing bomb threats.

Search Techniques

When a bomb threat is received, conducting a thorough and systematic search becomes paramount. The success of these searches hinges on the methodology, the tools used, and the coordination among team members. This section will explore the key techniques and best practices for conducting effective searches, ensuring you are well-prepared to handle such high-stakes situations.

Visual Inspection

The initial step in any search is a detailed visual inspection. This involves systematically scanning the area for any unusual items or disturbances. Here's how to execute a comprehensive visual inspection:

- **Methodical Approach**: Divide the area into sections and search each systematically. This ensures that no part of the area is overlooked.

- **High-Risk Areas**: Focus on high-risk areas such as entry points, lobbies, restrooms, trash bins, and under furniture. These are common places where a device might be hidden.

- **Patterns and Anomalies**: Look for items that seem out of place or anything that appears to have been tampered with. Pay close attention to any suspicious packages, bags, or devices.

Systematic Search Techniques

Conducting a systematic search involves a structured approach to ensure thorough coverage of the area. Here are key techniques to employ:

- **Grid Search**: Divide the area into a grid and assign each section to a specific team member. This technique ensures that each part of the area is covered without duplication.

- **Zonal Search**: Assign team members to specific zones based on their familiarity with the area. This can speed up the search and improve efficiency.

- **High and Low Searches**: Bombs can be placed at any height, so searchers must inspect high (ceilings, light fixtures) and low (under desks, furniture) locations.

Use of Specialized Equipment

Leveraging specialized equipment can enhance the thoroughness and safety of your search. Here are some tools that might be used:

- **Metal Detectors**: These are useful for identifying hidden devices that contain metal components.

- **Portable X-Ray Machines**: Often used to inspect suspicious packages without opening them.

- **Bomb-Sniffing Dogs**: Highly trained canines can detect explosive materials by scent, adding an invaluable layer of safety and effectiveness to the search.

Avoiding Disturbance

If a suspicious item is found, it's crucial not to disturb it. Here's how to handle such discoveries:

- **Do Not Touch**: Never touch or move a suspicious item. Disturbing, it could trigger an explosive device.

- **Establish a Perimeter**: Immediately set up a secure perimeter around the item. Ensure that this perimeter is well beyond its immediate vicinity to protect against potential blasts.

- **Notify Authorities**: Contact the bomb squad and law enforcement without delay. Provide them with detailed information about the item's appearance and location.

Searching High and Low

Ensure that the search includes all potential hiding places at eye level and beyond. Here's what to consider:

- **Ceilings and Light Fixtures**: Inspect areas above eye level, including ceilings, light fixtures, and ventilation systems.

- **Under Furniture**: Pay attention to areas under desks, chairs, and other furniture. These can be prime spots for hiding devices.

- **Hidden Compartments**: Be aware of hidden compartments or spaces that might be used to conceal a device.

Communication

Maintaining constant communication with team members and superiors during the search is essential. Here's how to ensure effective communication:

- **Two-Way Radios**: Use two-way radios to stay in contact with your team. Ensure that all communication is clear and concise.

- **Status Updates**: Regularly update your team and superiors on the status of the search. This helps coordinate efforts and ensure that all areas are covered.

- **Emergency Protocols**: Establish clear protocols for reporting and escalating findings. This ensures that any discovery is handled expeditiously and appropriately.

Safety Precautions

Safety should always be the top priority during a search. Here are key precautions to take:

- **Protective Gear**: Ensure that all personnel involved in the search are equipped with appropriate protective gear.

- **Evacuation Routes**: Be aware of evacuation routes and ensure they are clear. This is crucial in case a quick exit is necessary.

- **First Aid Readiness**: Have first aid kits readily available and ensure that team members are trained in basic first aid.

Practical Examples

Example of a Grid Search: Imagine you are searching a large conference center. Divide the space into a grid, assigning each square to a specific team member. This ensures comprehensive coverage without redundancy. Each member reports their findings, ensuring that no area is overlooked.

Example of Using Bomb-Sniffing Dogs: In a high-stakes scenario, deploying bomb-sniffing dogs can significantly enhance the effectiveness of the search. These dogs can quickly cover large areas and detect even well-hidden explosives, providing an additional layer of safety.

Commonalities in Search Techniques

Despite the various methods, some common principles apply to all search techniques:

- **Thoroughness**: Ensure that every part of the area is searched comprehensively.

- **Coordination**: Maintain clear communication and coordination among team members to avoid gaps in the search.

- **Documentation**: Document the search process, including areas covered and any findings. This information is vital for post-incident analysis.

Reflection and Continuous Improvement

After each search, conduct a thorough debrief to evaluate the effectiveness of your techniques and identify areas for improvement:

- **What Worked Well?**: Identify the strengths in your search strategy.

- **Areas for Improvement**: Determine what could have been done better and update your protocols accordingly.

- **Training Needs**: Implement additional training or drills based on lessons learned to ensure continuous improvement in your search capabilities.

Conducting effective searches during a bomb threat requires a combination of thoroughness, methodical techniques, and safety precautions. Mastering these techniques can significantly enhance the safety and security of your environment.

As we move into the next section on organized search methods, consider this: Are your current search techniques comprehensive and well-practiced? Do you and your team feel confident in your ability to conduct thorough and safe searches? Let's build on this foundation and explore organized search methods that further bolster your capabilities in managing bomb threats.

Organized Search Methods

In the event of a bomb threat, an organized search is critical to ensuring the safety and security of all individuals involved. While individual search techniques are important, a coordinated, team-based approach maximizes efficiency and effectiveness. Next, we will explore the structured methods that security personnel and bomb squads employ to thoroughly and safely search for potential explosive devices.

Coordination with the Bomb Squad

When a credible bomb threat is received, the first step is to contact the bomb squad. These experts have the training and equipment necessary to handle explosive devices safely. Here's how to coordinate effectively:

- **Immediate Notification**: Inform the bomb squad as soon as a suspicious item is discovered. Provide them with detailed information about the threat, including the location and description of the item.

- **Information Sharing**: Share all available information, such as facility blueprints, evacuation plans, and preliminary findings from your initial search. This information is crucial for the bomb squad's assessment and planning.

Initial Security Officer Role

Before the bomb squad arrives, security officers play a crucial role in the preliminary assessment and management of the situation. Here's what to do:

- **Preliminary Search**: Conduct a quick, visual search to identify any obvious threats. Use caution and avoid touching any suspicious items.

- **Evacuation Management**: If a threat is identified, initiate evacuation procedures immediately. Ensure that all individuals move to designated safe areas calmly and efficiently.

- **Perimeter Security**: Establish and maintain a secure perimeter around the suspicious item to prevent unauthorized access and protect against potential explosions.

Dividing the Search Area

The area should be divided into manageable sections to ensure a thorough search. Here's how to organize the search effectively:

- **Section Allocation**: Divide the facility into specific zones, assigning each zone to a team of security personnel and bomb squad members. This division ensures that every part of the area is covered without overlap.

- **Team Leaders**: Each team should have a designated leader responsible for coordinating the search within their assigned zone and reporting findings to the central command.

Methodical Search

A systematic approach to searching each zone ensures thoroughness. Here are some key practices:

- **Detailed Inspection**: Teams should perform a detailed inspection of their assigned zones, checking all potential hiding places for explosive devices, including ceilings, light fixtures, under furniture, and inside trash bins.

- **Use of Equipment**: Deploy specialized methods and equipment, such as bomb-sniffing dogs, metal detectors, and portable X-ray machines, to aid in the search. These tools can more effectively identify hidden or disguised devices.

Evacuation and Access Control

During the search, maintaining control over the evacuated area is essential. Here's how to manage evacuation and access:

- **Clear Routes**: Ensure that evacuation routes are clear and individuals move quickly and calmly to designated safe areas.

- **Access Restrictions**: Establish barriers and monitor entry points to prevent unauthorized access to the search zones.

Only authorized personnel should be allowed near the suspected area.

Documentation

Accurate search process documentation is crucial for immediate action and future reference. Here's what to document:

- **Search Logs**: Keep detailed logs of the search process, including times, locations searched, and findings. This information is vital for coordinating the search and for post-incident analysis.

- **Incident Reports**: After the search, compile comprehensive incident reports that include all relevant details. These reports are essential for legal purposes, insurance claims, and improving future response protocols.

Post-Search Debrief

After the search is complete, conducting a thorough debrief with all involved personnel helps evaluate the response's effectiveness and identify areas for improvement. Here's what to include in the debrief:

- **Review of Actions**: Discuss the steps taken during the search, highlighting what worked well and could be improved.

- **Lessons Learned**: Identify key lessons from the incident and use these insights to refine search protocols and training programs.

- **Future Training**: Implement additional training sessions based on the debrief findings to ensure continuous improvement in search techniques and coordination.

Practical Examples

Example of Coordinated Search in a Large Office Building: Imagine a bomb threat in a high-rise office building. The bomb squad arrives and coordinates with the building's security team. The building is divided into floors, with each floor assigned to a specific team. Bomb-sniffing dogs are deployed alongside security personnel using metal detectors. The teams methodically search each floor, reporting their findings to the command center. Evacuated personnel are kept in designated safe areas, and clear communication ensures that everyone is informed and calm. After a thorough search, no explosive devices are found, and the building is declared safe.

Example of Evacuation and Access Control in a Shopping Mall: A suspicious package is found in a busy shopping mall. Security officers quickly establish a perimeter and begin evacuating the mall, directing shoppers to safe exits and assembly points. The bomb squad arrives and divides the mall into sections for a detailed search. Security personnel assist in controlling access, ensuring that only authorized personnel enter the search zones. The search is documented meticulously, and after the threat is neutralized, a debrief session identifies strengths and areas for improvement in the response.

Reflection and Continuous Improvement

Reflecting on each search and continuously improving your methods is crucial for maintaining high standards of safety and efficiency:

- **Strengths and Weaknesses**: Identify the strengths in your search strategy and areas that need improvement.

- **Protocol Refinement**: Adjust your search protocols based on lessons learned to enhance future responses.

- **Ongoing Training**: Implement regular training sessions to keep skills sharp and ensure that all personnel are familiar with the latest search techniques and equipment.

Organized search methods are essential for effectively managing bomb threats. By coordinating with bomb squads, systematically dividing search areas, and maintaining clear communication and documentation, security personnel can ensure thorough and safe searches.

As we move to the final section of this chapter, where we will consolidate our learnings and reflect on the principles of bomb threat management, consider this: Are your current organized search methods comprehensive and well-practiced? Do you and your team feel confident in your ability to conduct thorough and coordinated searches? Let's solidify these practices and ensure your response to bomb threats is as effective and efficient as possible.

Key Takeaways and Final Reflection

As we conclude this comprehensive exploration of bomb threat and incident response management, it is crucial to consolidate the key learnings from each section. This reflection will help reinforce the essential principles and practices that can significantly improve bomb threat management.

The Importance of Pre-Planning

One of the fundamental lessons from this chapter is the absolute necessity of thorough preparation. "Effective response to bomb threats begins with thorough preparation. Knowing the facility's layout, establishing clear communication channels, and having well-practiced evacuation plans are essential." Pre-planning involves:

- **Facility Familiarity**: Understanding every aspect of the facility's layout, from exits to high-risk areas.

- **Communication Protocols**: Setting up clear, reliable lines of communication with internal teams and external authorities.

- **Regular Drills**: Conducting evacuation drills and training sessions to ensure readiness.

The effectiveness of your response hinges on the groundwork laid during these preparatory stages.

Roles and Responsibilities

Each member of the bomb management team has a specific role to play. Understanding and executing these roles efficiently ensures a coordinated and effective response:

- **Security Officers**: First responders who assess threats, manage evacuations, and secure perimeters.

- **Bomb Squad**: Specialists who handle and neutralize explosive devices.

- **Emergency Services**: Provide medical aid, fire control, and assist in evacuations.

- **Facility Management**: Supply critical infrastructure information and assist in post-incident recovery.

- **Communication Center**: Coordinate information flow and resource allocation.

- **Administrative Staff**: Notify stakeholders and maintain records.

Evaluating Threats

Assessing the credibility of a bomb threat is a critical skill. It involves:

- **Initial Assessment**: Quickly gathering details about the threat's specifics.

- **Information Gathering**: Engaging with the source of the threat and preserving evidence.

- **Consulting Experts**: Working closely with law enforcement and bomb squads.

- **Decision Making**: Determining whether to evacuate based on the threat's credibility and potential risk.

Handling Unattended vs. Suspicious Packages

Distinguishing between unattended and suspicious packages is crucial:

- **Unattended Packages**: Often benign but require careful assessment and adherence to protocol.

- **Suspicious Packages**: Exhibit signs of potential danger and necessitate immediate action, including establishing a perimeter and notifying authorities.

Search Techniques

Effective search techniques are the backbone of a thorough and safe bomb threat response:

- **Visual Inspection**: Methodically scan the area for unusual items.

- **Systematic Approach**: Use grid or zonal search methods to ensure complete coverage.

- **Specialized Equipment**: Employ tools like bomb-sniffing dogs and metal detectors.

- **Communication**: Maintain constant, clear communication among team members.

Organized Search Methods

An organized, team-based search maximizes efficiency and safety:

- **Coordination with Bomb Squad**: Ensure seamless collaboration with specialists.

- **Dividing the Search Area**: Assign specific zones to teams to prevent overlap.

- **Detailed Inspection**: Thoroughly inspect each assigned zone.

- **Documentation**: Keep accurate records of the search process and findings.

Continuous Improvement

"Every bomb threat, whether a false alarm or a genuine crisis, offers an opportunity for reflection and learning." Post-incident evaluations are essential:

- **Debriefing**: Review actions taken, identify strengths and weaknesses, and refine protocols.

- **Training**: Implement regular training sessions based on lessons learned to enhance readiness.

Conclusion

Bomb threat and incident response management is a dynamic and critical aspect of security work. The strategies and protocols outlined in this chapter are designed to equip you with the knowledge and skills needed to respond effectively to these high-stakes situations. By understanding the importance of preparation, clearly defining roles and responsibilities, evaluating threats accurately, and employing thorough search techniques, you can significantly enhance the safety and security of your environment.

As you move forward, consider this: How can you apply these principles to your daily routine to ensure constant readiness? Are your current protocols up to date and practiced regularly? Reflect on these questions and use the insights gained from this chapter to strengthen your approach to bomb threat management.

Staying vigilant, prepared, and informed is paramount in the ever-evolving security landscape. Your commitment to mastering these skills protects those you serve and elevates the standards of the entire security profession. Let's ensure that every response to a bomb threat is met with confidence, precision, and unwavering dedication to safety.

Chapter Six

Fire Safety

FIRE SAFETY IS CRITICAL to security work, encompassing much more than responding to fire alarms. It involves a proactive approach to preventing fires, recognizing hazards, and preparing for emergencies. As a security officer, your role in fire safety is pivotal. You are the first line of defense, preventing a small issue from becoming catastrophic.

Identifying Fire Hazards

Imagine walking through your workplace and noticing a sparking outlet or flammable materials improperly stored. These are not just minor issues but potential fire hazards waiting to cause a disaster. Regularly inspecting your environment for such risks is essential. Overloaded electrical outlets can spark and start fires. Flammable materials need to be stored correctly, away from heat sources. Blocked escape routes can prevent people from getting out safely in an emergency. By identifying and addressing these hazards, you can significantly reduce the risk of fire.

Fire Detection Systems

The importance of smoke alarms and sprinkler systems are not just equipment; they are lifesavers. Understanding and maintaining these systems is crucial. When they work correctly, they provide the first line of defense, alerting everyone to the danger and allowing for a timely response. "A study published in the Journal of Fire Sciences (2020) found that regular maintenance and testing of fire detection systems significantly improve their reliability and effectiveness in real fire scenarios." Regular checks and maintenance ensure these systems function properly when needed most.

Evacuation Procedures

A well-practiced fire drill where everyone knows exactly what to do and where to go will result in a smooth, calm, and efficient evacuation. Security officers must be familiar with evacuation procedures and routes in their assigned areas. Therefore, fire drills ensure that security personnel and building occupants know what to do in a fire. Clear signage and well-lit escape routes are essential. In the chaos of a real fire, this preparation can save lives. "In a fire, a well-practiced emergency response and evacuation plan can be the difference between safety and catastrophe."

Legal and Ethical Responsibilities

As a security officer, you must uphold fire safety standards. This means adhering to local fire codes, conducting regular safety checks, and ensuring fire safety equipment is accessible and functional. It's not just about compliance; it's about protecting lives. Neglecting these duties can have severe consequences, both legally and ethically.

Impact on Business and Community

Fires can devastate businesses and communities. Beyond the immediate threat to life and property, fires can lead to business interruptions, job losses, and community displacement. "The economic impact of fire incidents in the U.S. in 2019 was estimated at $14.8 billion, highlighting the importance of effective fire prevention and response strategies." Therefore, a proactive approach to fire safety is vital. By preventing fires, you protect not only the physical assets but also the livelihoods and well-being of many people.

Proactive Measures

Some practical steps you can take to enhance fire safety in your workplace are as follows: Start by conducting regular inspections. Look for potential hazards like faulty wiring, flammable materials, and blocked exits. Educate your colleagues about the importance of fire safety. Ensure everyone knows how to use fire extinguishers and where the emergency exits are.

Maintain all fire safety equipment regularly. Ensure smoke alarms and sprinkler systems are tested regularly and kept in good working order. Develop and regularly update a comprehensive fire safety plan. This plan should include evacuation routes, assembly points, and contact information for local fire departments.

Scenario I

Consider a day in a busy office building, during a routine inspection, you notice that boxes of office supplies block a fire exit. You immediately report this to the building management, who clears the obstruction. A week later, a small fire breaks out in the building. Thanks to the cleared fire exit and the building's well-practiced evacuation plan, all occupants are able to exit safely and quickly, and the fire is contained with minimal damage. This practical example illustrates the importance of vigilance and proactive fire safety measures.

As we conclude this section, remember that fire safety is not just about responding to emergencies but preventing them. Your proactive efforts in identifying hazards, maintaining detection systems, and preparing for emergencies can save lives and protect property. Stay vigilant, stay prepared, and prioritize fire safety in your role as a security officer. Your actions can significantly affect the safety and well-being of everyone in your workplace.

Fire Chemistry

Understanding the chemistry of fire is essential for anyone involved in fire safety. This knowledge helps prevent fires and effectively respond to them when they occur. The fire triangle is at the heart of this understanding: heat, fuel, and oxygen. Each element is necessary for a fire to start and sustain.

Elements of Fire

Heat Sources

Heat is the initial spark that starts a fire. It can come from various sources, such as open flames, electrical faults, friction, or chemical reactions. As a security officer, you should be aware of potential heat sources in your environment and manage them accordingly. For instance, electrical faults are a common cause of fires. Ensuring that electrical systems are regularly inspected and maintained can prevent overheating and sparks that could ignite a fire.

Fuel Types

Fuel is any material that can burn. This includes solid materials like wood and paper, liquids like gasoline, and gases. The nature of the fuel influences how a fire behaves and spreads. For example, paper and wood burn quickly and produce much heat, while liquids like gasoline can cause explosive fires. Understanding the types of fuel in your environment helps you assess and implement appropriate measures.

Oxygen

Oxygen is the component that sustains a fire. Air contains about 21% oxygen, which is sufficient to keep a fire burning. In enclosed spaces, limiting the oxygen supply can effectively suppress a fire from spreading. This is why fire suppression systems often include methods to reduce oxygen levels around a fire—for example, CO_2

extinguishers work by displacing oxygen and suffocating the flames.

The Fire Tetrahedron

Beyond the basic fire triangle, some fires involve a chemical chain reaction, adding a fourth element to form the fire tetrahedron. This concept is essential for dealing with complex fire scenarios where the fire might not be quickly extinguished by removing just one element of the fire triangle. Understanding this helps you choose the right fire suppression methods and equipment.

Practical Examples

Consider a location in an office building where an electrical fault causes fire; the heat from the faulty wiring ignites nearby paper documents (fuel), and the fire quickly spreads due to the ample supply of oxygen in the room. Recognizing the fire triangle elements in this situation allows the security officer to take appropriate actions, such as using a $CO2$ extinguisher to displace the oxygen and stop the fire.

Preventive Measures

To prevent fires, it's essential to manage heat sources, control fuel availability, and understand the role of oxygen. Here are some practical steps:

- **Regular Inspections**: Conduct regular inspections to identify and mitigate potential heat sources and ensure electrical systems are up to code and fault-free.

- **Proper Storage**: Store flammable materials in designated, secure areas away from potential ignition sources. Use fire-resistant containers and follow storage guidelines.

- **Ventilation Control**: In areas where fires are more likely, ensure that ventilation systems can be controlled to limit oxygen flow in case of a fire.

Understanding fire chemistry is crucial for effective fire safety. By knowing how heat, fuel, and oxygen interact to create and sustain fires, you can take proactive steps to prevent fires and respond effectively when they occur. Stay informed about the elements of fire and their implications for your environment. This knowledge will empower you to enhance fire safety measures and protect lives and property in your workplace.

Next, we'll explore the different classes of fire and the appropriate extinguishing methods for each. This knowledge is essential for ensuring that you use the right tools and techniques to combat fires effectively.

Classes of Fire

Different types of fires require different responses. Knowing the various classes of fires and the appropriate extinguishing methods is crucial for effective fire safety management. Let's explore the different classes of fire and how to handle them.

Class A: Combustibles

Class A fires involve common combustibles like wood, paper, plastic, and cloth. These materials burn easily and are found in many environments. To extinguish a Class A fire, you can use a bucket of water or fully pressurized water-based extinguishers, which will cool the burning material and prevent re-ignition.

Scenario II

Consider a scene in an office building where a stack of paper catches fire due to a discarded cigarette. The security officer quickly grabs a fully pressurized water extinguisher and sprays the base of the flames, effectively cooling and extinguishing the fire. This swift action prevents the fire from spreading to other combustible materials in the area.

Class B: Flammable Liquids

Flammable liquids like gasoline, oil, and solvents cause class B fires. These fires require foam, dry chemicals, or CO_2 extinguishers. Using water on Class B fires can be dangerous because it can spread the flammable liquid, worsening the fire.

Scenario III

In a workshop, a can of gasoline is accidentally knocked over, and the liquid ignites. The security officer uses a foam extinguisher to cover the flames, creating a barrier between the fire and the fuel source.

This action stops the fire from spreading and brings it under control.

Class C: Electrical Fires

Class C fires involve electrical equipment. They require non-conductive extinguishing agents like CO_2 or dry chemical extinguishers. To prevent electrical shock, it's also crucial to cut off the power source before attempting to extinguish the fire.

Scenario IV

An electrical panel in a data center catches fire due to a short circuit. The security officer quickly shuts off the power and uses a CO_2 extinguisher to put out the flames. By using the appropriate extinguisher, the officer avoids the risk of electrical shock and prevents further damage to the equipment.

Class D: Metal Fires

Class D fires involve combustible metals such as magnesium, titanium, and sodium. These fires require special extinguishing agents like dry powder, which are designed to handle high-temperature fires without reacting with the metals.

Scenario V

A small amount of magnesium shavings caught fire in a manufacturing plant. The security officer used a Class D extinguisher to safely extinguish the fire, preventing it from spreading to other areas of the plant.

Class K: Kitchen Fires

Class K fires are common in household and commercial kitchens and involve cooking oils and fats. Wet chemical extinguishers are specifically designed for these types of fires. They work by creating a foam layer that cools and suppresses the heat in oils or fats.

Scenario VI

A deep fryer full of hot oil catches fire in a restaurant kitchen. The chef quickly uses a wet chemical extinguisher to spray the burning oil, forming a foam layer that cools the oil's heat and prevents the fire from spreading. This quick response ensures the safety of the kitchen staff and patrons.

Research Insights

Research into the effectiveness of various fire extinguishers demonstrates that having the appropriate extinguisher type for different classes of fire significantly enhances fire suppression success rates[1]. Knowing which extinguisher to use and how to use it properly can make a critical difference in an emergency.

Training and Familiarization

To ensure effective fire response, security officers must be trained and familiar with the different types of fire extinguishers available in their workplace. Regular training sessions and drills can help reinforce this knowledge and ensure readiness in case of a fire.

Understanding the different classes of fire and the appropriate extinguishing methods is essential for effective fire safety management. By knowing how to respond to each type of fire, you can protect lives and property more effectively. Stay informed, stay prepared, and ensure that you and your team are equipped with the right tools and knowledge to handle any fire emergency. Next, we'll discuss the risks associated with hazardous materials in the workplace and how to manage them safely.

Hazardous Materials

Hazardous materials in the workplace can significantly increase the risk and severity of fires. Understanding and managing these risks is key to maintaining a safe environment. Security officers should familiarize themselves with their company policy on how to handle hazardous materials effectively to prevent fire incidents by contacting the appropriate emergency responders to handle the incident swiftly.

Storage and Handling

Proper storage and handling of hazardous materials are essential. Here's how you can ensure safety:

- **Designated Storage Areas**: Hazardous materials should be stored in well-ventilated areas away from heat sources. These areas should be marked with clear signage indicating the presence of hazardous materials.

- **Proper Labeling**: Each container of hazardous materials should be clearly labeled with its contents and associated hazards. This helps in identifying the materials quickly during an emergency and ensures that everyone knows what they are handling.

- **Secure Containers**: Use appropriate containers for storing hazardous materials. These containers should be durable, sealed, and resistant to the materials they hold. Properly sealing containers prevents leaks and spills that could lead to fires.

Scenario VII

Consider a laboratory where various chemicals are used daily. In this lab, chemicals are stored in a designated, well-ventilated storage room. Each container is clearly labeled, and incompatible chemicals are stored separately to prevent reactions. By following these best practices, the lab minimizes the risk of fire and ensures a safe working environment.

Emergency Response

In the event of a fire involving hazardous materials, special procedures are required. Here's how to handle such situations:

- **Evacuation**: Immediately evacuate the area to ensure the safety of all personnel. Follow the established evacuation routes and assembly points. Make sure everyone knows these procedures in advance through regular drills.

- **Containment**: If it is safe to do so, secure the area by closing doors to prevent the fire from spreading.

- **Coordination with Specialized Teams**: Work closely with specialized response teams, such as the fire department and hazardous materials (HazMat) units. These teams have the expertise and equipment to handle such incidents safely, and clear communication with them is crucial for a coordinated response.

Material Safety Data Sheets (MSDS)

Familiarity with Material Safety Data Sheets (MSDS) is crucial. These sheets provide detailed information on the handling and risks associated with hazardous materials. Here's why they are important:

- **Information Access**: MSDS provides vital information on the properties of hazardous materials, including their flammability, reactivity, and toxicity. This information is essential for safe handling and emergency response.

- **Emergency Procedures**: They outline specific procedures for handling spills, fires, and other emergencies involving the materials. Knowing these procedures can make a difference in an emergency situation.

- **Health and Safety Guidelines**: MSDS includes guidelines on the proper use of personal protective equipment (PPE) and first aid measures in case of exposure. Ensuring that all personnel are familiar with these guidelines is critical for their safety.

Scenario VIII

In a factory, a security officer encounters a leaking container of a hazardous chemical. By quickly referencing the MSDS, the officer learns that the chemical is highly flammable and takes appropriate measures to contain the spill and evacuate the area. The MSDS also provides instructions on the use of PPE to safely manage the incident, highlighting the importance of these documents in ensuring safety.

Training and Awareness

To effectively manage hazardous materials, all personnel must be trained and aware of the associated risks and safety procedures. Here are some training tips:

- **Regular Training Sessions**: Conduct regular training sessions on the proper storage, handling, and emergency response procedures for hazardous materials. Keeping everyone informed and trained can prevent accidents.

- **Drills and Simulations**: Incorporate drills and simulations into the training program to provide hands-on experience in managing hazardous material incidents. Practice makes perfect, and being prepared can save lives.

- **Access to Information**: Ensure that all personnel have easy access to MSDS and understand how to use them. Having this information readily available is essential for quick and effective responses.

Preventive Measures

Preventing incidents involving hazardous materials requires proactive measures. Here are some strategies:

- **Regular Inspections**: Conduct regular inspections of storage areas and containers to ensure they are in good condition and comply with safety standards. Identifying potential problems early can prevent accidents.

- **Risk Assessments**: Perform risk assessments to identify potential hazards and implement measures to mitigate them. Understanding the risks allows you to take appropriate actions to minimize them.

- **Maintenance of Safety Equipment**: Ensure that safety equipment, such as fire extinguishers and spill containment kits, is readily available and in good working condition. Regular maintenance is essential for ensuring it works when needed.

Research Insights

"A study published in the Journal of Fire Sciences found that regular maintenance and testing of fire detection systems significantly improve their reliability and effectiveness in real fire scenarios." This insight emphasizes the importance of keeping safety equipment in top condition to prevent and respond to fires involving hazardous materials.

Conclusion

Managing hazardous materials is a critical aspect of fire safety. By following proper storage and handling procedures, familiarizing yourself with the Material Safety Data Sheet (MSDS), and conducting regular training and inspections, you can significantly reduce the risk of fires and ensure a safe working environment. Safety is everyone's responsibility, and staying vigilant can prevent disasters.

Next, we'll discuss the different types of fire extinguishers and their specific uses. This knowledge is essential for choosing the right tool to combat fires effectively.

Types of Fire Extinguishers

Fire extinguishers are vital tools in combating fires, but using the right type for the specific fire class is essential. Understanding the various types of fire extinguishers and their uses ensures you can respond effectively to different fire scenarios. Below are different types of fire extinguishers and their specific uses:

Halotron Fire Extinguisher

The clean agent halotron is one of the most widely used fire extinguishers. It is used for class A, B, and C fires caused by ordinary combustible materials such as wood, cloth, plastic, and paper. This extinguisher is also used to fight fires caused by flammable liquids such as gasoline, propane, grease, and oil. Halotron fire extinguishers are also very effective in combating electrical fires.

Water Extinguishers

Water extinguishers are ideal for Class A fires involving materials like wood, paper, and textiles. They work by cooling the burning material, which prevents re-ignition. However, they should not be used on electrical fires or flammable liquids, as water can spread the flames or cause electrical shocks.

Scenario IX

Imagine a small fire in an office. A wastebasket filled with paper catches fire. A security officer quickly grabs a water extinguisher and sprays the base of the flames, effectively cooling and extinguishing the fire. This quick action prevents the fire from spreading to nearby office supplies and furniture.

Foam Extinguishers

Foam extinguishers are effective on Class A and B fires involving flammable liquids like gasoline, oil, grease, paint, or solvents. They create a barrier between the fire and the fuel source, smothering the flames. However, care should be taken with electrical equipment, as foam can conduct electricity.

Scenario X

A small fire starts in a garage due to a gasoline spill that ignites. The security officer uses a foam extinguisher to cover the flames, creating a barrier between the fire and the gasoline. This action stops the fire from spreading and brings it under control.

Dry Chemical Extinguishers

Dry chemical extinguishers are versatile and suitable for Class A, B, and C fires. They work by interrupting the fire's chemical reaction, making them a common choice for various environments. However, they can leave a residue that needs to be cleaned up after use.

Scenario XI

An electrical fire starts in a workshop due to a faulty power tool. The security officer quickly shuts off the power and uses a dry chemical extinguisher to put out the flames. The extinguisher effectively stops the fire without the risk of electrical shock.

Carbon Dioxide (CO2) Extinguishers

CO2 extinguishers are best for Class B and electrical fires. They work by displacing oxygen and cooling the fire. CO2 extinguishers don't leave any residue, making them ideal for offices and areas with electronic equipment.

Scenario XII

An electrical panel in a server room caught fire. The security officer grabbed a CO_2 extinguisher and sprayed the base of the flames, displacing the oxygen and heat from the fire. This action quickly extinguished the fire without damaging the electronic equipment.

Wet Chemical Extinguishers

Wet chemical extinguishers are specifically designed for Class K fires involving cooking oils and fats. They work by creating a foam layer that cools and smothers the burning oils or fats. These extinguishers are commonly found in commercial kitchens.

Scenario XIII

In a restaurant kitchen, a deep fryer full of hot oil catches fire. The chef quickly uses a wet chemical extinguisher to spray the burning oil, forming a foam layer that cools the oil and prevents the fire from spreading. This quick response ensures the safety of the kitchen staff and patrons.

Dry Powder

Dry powder is used to fight class D combustible metal fires. Some combustible metals include zinc, aluminum, sodium, titanium, and potassium. It is also effective in fighting lithium fire. They are often used in metal shaving shops.

Pull, Aim, Squeeze and Sweep (PASS) Technique

Knowing how to use a fire extinguisher correctly is just as important as having the right type. The PASS technique is a simple method for using an extinguisher effectively:

- **Pull the Pin**: This unlocks the operating lever and allows you to discharge the extinguisher.

- **Aim at the Base of the Fire**: Target the source of the flames, not the flames themselves.

- **Squeeze the Handle**: This releases the extinguishing agent.

- **Sweep Side to Side**: Move the extinguisher nozzle back and forth to cover the fire's entire base.

Research Insights

"Research into the effectiveness of various fire extinguishers demonstrates that having the appropriate extinguisher type for different classes of fire significantly enhances fire suppression success rates." This research underscores the importance of equipping your workplace with the right extinguishers and training personnel on their proper use.

Training and Familiarization

To ensure effective fire response, security officers must be trained and familiar with the different types of fire extinguishers available in their workplace. Regular training sessions and drills can help reinforce this knowledge and ensure readiness in case of a fire. Here's how to implement effective training:

- **Hands-On Training**: Provide hands-on training sessions where personnel can practice using different types of extinguishers.

- **Regular Drills**: Conduct regular fire drills that include using fire extinguishers as part of the emergency response.

- **Information Access**: Ensure that all personnel have access to information on the different types of extinguishers and their specific uses.

Understanding the different types of fire extinguishers and their appropriate uses is essential for effective fire safety management. By knowing how to respond to each type of fire, you can protect lives and property more effectively. Equip your workplace with the right extinguishers, ensure regular maintenance, and provide comprehensive training to all personnel. Stay informed, stay prepared, and ensure that you and your team are equipped with the right tools and knowledge to handle any fire emergency.

The next section will discuss the steps to extinguish small fires safely and effectively. This knowledge will further enhance your ability to manage fire incidents and protect your workplace. Let's continue building your fire safety expertise.

Extinguishing Small Fires

A security officer's actions can prevent a larger disaster when faced with a small fire. Knowing how to assess the situation, choose the right extinguisher, and use it effectively can make all the difference. Let's explore the steps to extinguish small fires and the best practices to follow safely.

Assessment

When encountering a fire, the first step is to assess its size and type quickly. If the fire is small and manageable, you may attempt to extinguish it. If it's spreading rapidly, produces thick smoke, or involves hazardous materials, it's best to evacuate immediately and call the fire department. Here's how to conduct a quick assessment:

- **Size and Spread**: Is the fire small and contained, or is it spreading quickly? Small fires are typically confined to a small area, like a wastebasket or stovetop.

- **Type of Fire**: Identify the type of fire (Class A, B, C, D, or K) to determine the appropriate extinguishing method. This is crucial for effective response.

- **Hazards**: Are there any immediate hazards, such as flammable liquids or electrical equipment, that could make the situation more dangerous?

Scenario XIV

A small fire started in a kitchen due to oil overheating on the stove. The fire was confined to the pan, and no flammable materials were nearby. The security officer quickly assessed the situation and determined that a Class K fire could be safely extinguished using a wet chemical extinguisher.

Ensuring Safety

While extinguishing a fire, maintain a safe distance and ensure there is an accessible escape route. Here are some safety tips to follow:

- **Maintain Distance**: Stand a safe distance from the fire, typically about 6-8 feet, and move closer only if necessary.

- **Accessible Escape Route**: Ensure you have a clear path to evacuate in case the fire becomes uncontrollable.

- **Monitor the Fire**: After extinguishing the fire, stay vigilant. Fires can reignite, especially if not completely extinguished.

After Extinguishing

Once the fire is out, take the following steps to ensure safety and address the aftermath:

- **Stay Vigilant**: Continue to monitor the area to ensure the fire does not reignite.

- **Ventilate the Area**: If possible, ventilate the area to clear any smoke and reduce inhalation risks.

- **Report the Incident**: Report the incident to your supervisor and document the details for future reference.

- **Check for Damage**: Assess the area for any damage and ensure that all fire safety equipment used is replenished and ready for future use.

Research Insights

"In 2019, the FBI reported over 1,000 bomb threats in the United States, highlighting the ongoing risk and necessity for effective response protocols." While this statistic pertains to bomb threats, it underscores the broader point that security threats are common, and preparedness is key. This includes being prepared to respond to small fires effectively.

Conclusion

Your quick assessment and appropriate action can prevent a larger disaster when faced with a small fire. By choosing the right extinguisher and using it correctly, you can effectively manage small fires and protect your workplace. Remember to maintain safety, ensure clear escape routes, and stay vigilant even after the fire is out. With these skills, you can significantly improve your ability to handle fire emergencies.

Next, we'll discuss the importance of personal safety when responding to fires. Knowing how to protect yourself in these situations is crucial.

Your Safety

Your safety is the top priority when responding to a fire. As a security officer, it's crucial to understand the risks involved and take appropriate measures to protect yourself while managing fire emergencies. Let's explore the keyaspects of personal safety during fire incidents and how to ensure you remain safe while performing your duties.

Risk Evaluation

Before taking any action, evaluate the risk involved. Assess the size of the fire, the type of materials burning, and the environment. If the fire is too large, produces toxic smoke, or involves hazardous materials, prioritize evacuation. Here's how to conduct a risk evaluation:

- **Fire Size and Spread**: Is the fire small and contained, or is it spreading rapidly? Large, uncontrollable fires require immediate evacuation.

- **Materials Involved**: Identify the burning materials. Fires involving hazardous substances, like chemicals or electrical equipment, pose additional risks.

- **Environmental Factors**: Consider factors such as ventilation, exit availability, and the presence of other hazards. Ensure you have a clear understanding of the environment before acting.

Scenario XV

In an industrial facility, a security officer notices a fire starting in a storage area containing flammable chemicals. Assessing the situation, the officer realizes the fire is too dangerous to tackle with a standard extinguisher. Prioritizing safety, the officer initiates an immediate evacuation and contacts emergency services, ensuring that all personnel are safely evacuated.

Protective Equipment

Using personal protective equipment (PPE) is essential, especially in situations involving smoke or hazardous materials. PPE can include gloves, masks, eye protection, and fire-resistant clothing. Here's how to use PPE effectively:

- **Gloves**: Protect your hands from burns and exposure to hazardous materials.

- **Masks**: Use masks to protect against smoke inhalation and toxic fumes. Respirators are recommended in environments with significant smoke or chemical exposure.

- **Eye Protection**: Wear goggles to protect your eyes from smoke, debris, and chemicals.

- **Fire-Resistant Clothing**: Wear appropriate clothing that can withstand heat and flames, reducing the risk of burns.

Smoke Awareness

Smoke inhalation is a major risk during fires. Be aware of the dangers and take steps to minimize exposure. Here's how to stay safe:

- **Stay Low**: In smoky conditions, stay low to the ground, where the air is clearer. Smoke rises, so crouching or crawling can help you avoid inhaling it.

- **Use Masks or Cloths**: If you don't have a mask, use a cloth to cover your mouth and nose to filter out smoke particles.

- **Ventilation**: If it is safe, ventilate the area by opening windows or doors to allow smoke to escape.

Scenario XVI

In a hotel fire, a security officer encounters thick smoke in the hallway. Remembering their training, the officer stays low to the ground, using a cloth to cover their mouth and nose while guiding guests to safety through a smoke-free exit route. This action minimizes smoke inhalation risks for everyone involved.

Heat and Fire Behavior

Understanding fire behavior and heat can help you make informed decisions during an emergency. Recognize signs of fire spread and structural weakness. Here's what to look for:

- **Heat Intensity**: If the heat is intense, it indicates the fire is large and dangerous. Avoid direct exposure and maintain a safe distance.

- **Fire Spread**: Observe how the fire is spreading. If it's moving quickly or involves flammable materials, prioritize evacuation.

- **Structural Weakness**: Be aware of signs that the structure is weakening, such as sagging floors, cracking walls, or loud popping sounds. These signs indicate an imminent collapse and immediate evacuation is necessary.

Scenario XVII

A security officer notices the fire spreading rapidly across several rooms in an office building. The heat becomes intense, and the officer hears cracking sounds from the ceiling. Recognizing the danger, the officer evacuates all occupants and moves them to a safe area outside the building.

Post-Incident Care

After responding to a fire, seek medical attention if necessary and participate in any debriefings to discuss what happened and how to improve future responses. Here's how to handle post-incident care:

- **Medical Attention**: Even if you feel fine, get checked by medical professionals for smoke inhalation or other injuries.

- **Debriefings**: Participate in debriefings with your team to review the incident. Discuss what went well and identify areas for improvement.

- **Mental Health**: Fire incidents can be traumatic. If needed, seek support from mental health professionals and encourage your team to do the same.

Scenario XVIII

After a fire incident at a warehouse, the security team undergoes medical evaluations for smoke inhalation. They then participate in a debriefing session, discussing their response and identifying ways to improve their procedures. The team also receives information on accessing mental health resources to address any stress or trauma from the incident.

Conclusion

Your safety is paramount when responding to a fire. You can protect yourself by evaluating risks, using protective equipment, understanding smoke and fire behavior, and seeking post-incident care while effectively managing fire emergencies. Remember, no property is worth more than your life. If the situation is beyond your control, evacuate and call for professional help.

As we conclude this chapter on fire safety, let's reflect on the importance of preparedness, proactive measures, and personal safety in fire management. Your role as a security officer is crucial in ensuring the safety and well-being of everyone in your workplace.

Stay vigilant, stay prepared, and always prioritize safety in your fire response efforts.

Comprehensive Risk Assessment

The foundation of effective fire safety is a thorough understanding of potential risks. This involves identifying fire hazards, assessing the likelihood of fire incidents, and evaluating their potential impact. Regular risk assessments are vital in maintaining an environment that minimally exposes occupants and properties to fire hazards.

Imagine conducting a detailed inspection of your workplace, identifying overloaded electrical outlets, improperly stored flammable materials, and blocked escape routes. Addressing these risks can significantly reduce the chances of a fire occurring. According to the National Fire Protection Association (NFPA), approximately 1,291,500 fires were reported in the United States in 2019[2]. This statistic highlights the importance of identifying and mitigating potential fire hazards to prevent such incidents.

Proactive Fire Prevention Measures

Prevention is always better than cure, especially in the context of fire safety. The preventive strategies outlined in this chapter—from maintaining fire safety equipment to implementing

---

2. National Fire Protection Association. (2019). *Approximately 1,291,500 fires reported in the United States in 2019:* https://www.nfpa.org

strict housekeeping practices—play a pivotal role in reducing the risk of fire. Adherence to building codes, proper storage of flammable materials, and regular maintenance of electrical systems are not just recommendations; they are non-negotiable practices that ensure safety.

Consider the impact of implementing a rigorous fire safety protocol in a commercial kitchen. Regularly cleaning grease from kitchen surfaces, properly storing flammable oils, and maintaining kitchen appliances can prevent the common causes of Class K fires. "The economic impact of fire incidents in the U.S. in 2019 was estimated at $14.8 billion, highlighting the importance of effective fire prevention and response strategies[3]." Preventive measures can save not only lives but also significant financial losses.

Emergency Response and Evacuation Plans

A well-practiced emergency response and evacuation plan can be the difference between safety and catastrophe in the event of a fire. The importance of having clear, accessible, and practiced evacuation routes cannot be overstated. Regular drills, clear signage, and an understanding of evacuation procedures are critical components of a robust fire safety strategy.

Imagine a fire drill where everyone knows their role and exits

---

3. National Fire Protection Association. (2019). *The economic impact of fire incidents in the U.S. in 2019 was estimated at $14.8 billion:* https://www.nfpa.org

the building calmly and efficiently. Such preparedness ensures that panic is minimized in a real emergency and evacuation is swift and safe. "In the event of a fire, a well-practiced emergency response and evacuation plan can be the difference between safety and catastrophe[4]." Regularly practicing these drills helps familiarize everyone with the procedures, ensuring they act quickly and efficiently when it matters most.

Training and Awareness

Knowledge and awareness are powerful tools in fire safety. Training in the use of fire extinguishers, understanding fire alarm systems, and recognizing fire hazards are fundamental in cultivating a safety-conscious environment.

Consider the value of hands-on training sessions where employees practice using fire extinguishers. By familiarizing themselves with the PASS technique (Pull the pin, Aim at the base of the fire, Squeeze the handle, and Sweep side to side), they gain the confidence and skills needed to respond effectively to a fire. A study published in the Journal of Fire Sciences found that regular maintenance and testing of fire detection systems significantly improve their reliability

---

4. *In the event of a fire, a well-practiced emergency response and evacuation plan can be the difference between safety and catastrophe. (2024):*

and effectiveness in real fire scenarios[5]. Continuous education and training ensure that everyone is prepared to act promptly and appropriately in an emergency.

Collaboration with Emergency Services

Effective fire safety management involves working closely with local fire departments and emergency services. This partnership ensures that the response to a fire is swift, coordinated, and efficient.

Consider the importance of conducting joint drills with local fire departments. These drills help familiarize emergency responders with your facility and its specific hazards, ensuring a seamless and effective response during an actual fire. Regular communication and collaboration with emergency services enhance your fire safety strategy and ensure that you are prepared for any situation.

Continuous Learning and Adaptation

Fire safety is an evolving field, with new challenges emerging as technologies and environments change. Staying updated with the latest fire safety standards, technologies, and best practices is crucial. An attitude of continuous learning and adaptation is essential for maintaining a safe and secure environment.

---

5. Journal of Fire Sciences. (2020). *Regular maintenance and testing of fire detection systems significantly improve their reliability and effectiveness in real fire scenarios:* https://www.fire-sciences.com

Imagine attending workshops and training sessions on the latest fire safety technologies and regulations. You can continuously improve your fire safety protocols by staying informed about advancements in fire detection systems, suppression methods, and safety standards. Embracing continuous learning ensures you are always equipped with the most effective tools and knowledge to protect your environment.

Reflecting on Key Takeaways

As we reflect on this chapter, let's summarize the key takeaways:

- **Be Prepared**: Knowledge and preparation are your first lines of defense. Regular training and detailed evacuation plans are crucial.

- **Act Swiftly and Decisively**: Quick, informed decisions can save lives. Evaluate threats promptly and communicate clearly.

- **Coordinate and Communicate**: Ensure seamless coordination among all team members and external agencies. Clear communication is essential for effective response.

- **Reflect and Improve**: Every incident is an opportunity to learn and improve. Continuous reflection and training are vital for maintaining high safety and efficiency standards.

Your role is pivotal in the realm of security. The actions you take, the decisions you make, and the preparations you implement can mean the difference between safety and disaster. Your readiness, vigilance, and commitment to continuous improvement make you a guardian of safety and a beacon of calm in crisis.

Are you prepared to face these challenges head-on? Will you continue to refine your skills and protocols to ensure the highest level of security for those you protect? The knowledge and strategies you've gained from this chapter should empower you to act with confidence and precision. Embrace this responsibility and make a difference.

Chapter Seven

Cargo Theft and Theft Prevention

In today's fast-paced world of logistics and transportation, cargo theft is a significant concern that disrupts businesses and impacts the global supply chain. This ongoing threat poses serious risks to the economic health of companies and the smooth flow of goods and services essential to our daily lives. As security officers, understanding the complexities of cargo theft is crucial for protecting assets and maintaining the integrity of the supply chain.

Cargo theft involves the unauthorized taking of goods during transit. These goods range from high-value electronics, which are highly sought after for their resale potential, to everyday items like food and construction materials. Theft can happen anywhere, from when goods leave the manufacturer until they arrive at a retail store or distribution center. This makes the role of a security officer multifaceted, requiring vigilance at loading docks, during transportation, and through collaboration with law enforcement.

In this chapter, we will explore the various aspects of cargo theft.

We'll start by defining what constitutes 'cargo' in the context of Theft and security. Understanding the broad spectrum of cargo helps create comprehensive protection strategies. We'll then explore the profile of a typical cargo thief, shedding light on their methods, motivations, and operations. This knowledge is vital for preempting potential thefts and implementing effective deterrents.

The tools and techniques cargo thieves use are diverse, ranging from physical tools used to break into containers or vehicles to sophisticated technological tools like GPS jammers and digital hacking systems. An in-depth understanding of these tools will equip you, as a security officer, with the knowledge to anticipate and counteract such threats.

Furthermore, we will identify the types of freight most commonly targeted by cargo thieves. Recognizing which cargoes are at higher risk allows for focused security measures and heightened vigilance where it matters most.

By the end of this chapter, you will have a thorough understanding of cargo theft and the measures necessary to prevent it. This knowledge is essential for protecting assets and ensuring the smooth operation of the global supply chain on which businesses and consumers rely.

Definition of Cargo

Cargo theft is a significant threat to businesses and the economy. To combat this menace effectively, it is essential to understand what constitutes 'cargo' and the complexities involved in its protection. This section will explore the definition of cargo in the context of security and examine the diverse range of goods and transportation methods involved.

What Is Cargo?

In security, cargo refers to goods or commodities transported for commercial gain. These goods range from raw materials like metals and grains to finished products like electronics and pharmaceuticals. The transportation methods for these goods are diverse, including trucks, rails, ships, and airplanes. Each mode of transport presents its own set of security challenges.

Think about the variety of items you encounter daily, from the smartphone in your pocket to the food on your table; most of these items have been part of a cargo shipment at some point. Recognizing the breadth of what cargo includes helps in comprehensively strategizing its protection.

Scenario I

Consider a truck loaded with high-end electronics traveling from a distribution center to various retail stores. This truck represents a prime target for cargo thieves because of its contents' high value and easy resale potential. Now, imagine a ship carrying bulk grains from one continent to another. While the goods may not have the same resale value as electronics, the cargo's sheer volume and essential nature make it a valuable target for thieves.

Security Challenges Across Different Transport Methods

Each transportation method has unique security challenges. For example:

- **Trucks**: Trucks are vulnerable during rest stops, loading, and unloading. Thieves often target trucks parked in isolated areas or those with visible high-value cargo.

- **Railcars**: Railcars can be targeted when stationary in rail yards or during transit through remote areas. The vast network of railroads makes it challenging to monitor every segment effectively.

- **Ships**: Ships face threats of piracy, especially in certain high-risk areas. Port security is also a concern, as cargo can be tampered with or stolen while waiting to be loaded or unloaded.

- **Airplanes**: While air cargo is generally more secure, it can still be targeted during ground handling and in less secure airports.

"Understanding the methods and motivations of cargo thieves is crucial for developing effective deterrents and prevention strategies[1]

---

1. *Understanding the methods and motivations of cargo thieves is crucial for developing effective deterrents and prevention strategies.* (2023): https://www.transportationsecurity.com

." According to recent statistics, cargo theft incidents increased by 16% in 2023, with electronics and pharmaceuticals being the most targeted items[2]. This statistic underscores the importance of being vigilant and proactive in safeguarding these valuable goods.

Understanding the broad definition of cargo and the diverse range of goods transported helps comprehensively strategize their protection. Recognizing the specific security challenges associated with different transport methods is the first step in developing effective deterrents and prevention strategies.

The Profile of a Typical Cargo Thief

Understanding who the thieves are and how they operate is essential to effectively preventing cargo theft. We will now examine the profile of a typical cargo thief and explore their methods, motivations, and operations.

Who Are Cargo Thieves?

Cargo thieves vary in sophistication and operation scale. They can be individuals looking for easy, opportunistic thefts or part of an organized crime group executing well-planned heists. Common characteristics include:

---

2. CargoNet. (2023). *Cargo theft incidents increased by 16% in 2023, with electronics and pharmaceuticals being the most targeted items:*

- **Knowledge of the System**: Many cargo thieves have inside knowledge of the transportation and logistics of the companies they are targeting, often gained from current employees or previous employment in the industry.

- **Use of Technology**: Experienced thieves use advanced technology and inside information to track shipments and identify valuable cargo.

- **Adaptability**: Cargo thieves can quickly adapt to changing security measures by employing lookouts, using police radar tracking systems, and exploiting new vulnerabilities.

Scenario II

In one instance, a group of thieves with detailed knowledge of the logistics system targeted a warehouse. They used stolen credentials to gain access, then systematically emptied the warehouse of high-value electronics. Their inside knowledge allowed them to bypass several layers of security, making the Theft highly efficient.

Motivations Behind Cargo Theft

The motivations behind cargo theft are typically financial. Thieves target goods that are easy to resell on the black market, such as electronics, pharmaceuticals, and branded apparel. The high value and demand for these items make them attractive targets.

Techniques and Tools Used

Cargo thieves employ a variety of tools and techniques:

- **Physical Tools**: These include bolt cutters, screwdrivers, lock picks, and crowbars used to break into containers or vehicles.

- **Technological Tools**: GPS jammers disrupt tracking devices, while hacking tools can compromise digital security systems.

- **Social Engineering**: Thieves may use false identities and documents to access cargo legally or gain information about shipment details.

Research Insights

Research published in the Journal of Transportation Security indicates that driver training programs focusing on situational awareness can decrease the likelihood of cargo theft by 25%[3]. An academic paper in the Journal of Supply Chain Management identified that regular security audits and risk assessments are crucial

---

3. Journal of Transportation Security. (2023). *Driver training programs focusing on situational awareness can decrease the likelihood of cargo theft by 25%:* https://www.journaloftransportationsecurity.com

in mitigating cargo theft risks[4].

Understanding the profile of a typical cargo thief, their motivations, and the tools they use is critical for developing effective security strategies. By recognizing these traits and techniques, security officers can better anticipate potential threats and implement measures to counteract them.

Types of Cargo Theft

Cargo theft manifests in various forms, each requiring specific preventive measures. Let's explore the common types of cargo theft and their unique challenges.

Armed Hijacking

Armed hijacking involves the use of force or the threat of force to take control of cargo vehicles. This type of Theft typically occurs in several stages:

- **Target Identification**: Hijackers often pre-select their targets based on the value of the cargo and the route's vulnerability.

- **Interception**: The hijackers intercept the vehicle in a location where they can avoid public attention.

---

4. Journal of Supply Chain Management. (2023). *Regular security audits and risk assessments are crucial in mitigating cargo theft risks:* https://www.journalofsupplychainmanagement.com

- **Seizure**: Using weapons to intimidate or incapacitate the driver, the hijackers take control of the vehicle.

- **Cargo Transfer**: The stolen cargo is quickly transferred to another vehicle or offloaded to a warehouse to avoid detection.

Impact and Prevention

Armed hijacking can lead to significant financial losses, increased insurance premiums, and supply chain disruptions. Prevention strategies include route planning, driver training, vehicle security enhancements, and cooperation with law enforcement.

Leaking

Leaking represents a more insidious form of cargo theft involving the gradual, often undetected, siphoning of goods from the supply chain. It involves stealing cargo without tampering with the seal. This type of theft typically involves insiders who steal the cargo before putting the seal on it. The major goal of the driver is to deliver the goods to the buyer with the seal intact, thereby preventing any type of suspicion from the buyer.

- **Modus Operandi**: Owners and employees within a company exploit their position to gradually divert goods before sealing the container.

- **Impact**: The cumulative loss of goods can amount to significant financial losses over time.

Prevention strategies focus on robust inventory management, employee screening, and fostering a culture of integrity and transparency.

Recouping

Recouping involves the Theft of cargo through the manipulation or exploitation of logistical processes. In recouping, delivery is based on the number of cartons to be delivered, and drivers are typically involved in opening cartons, taking some items, and sealing them back. The goal of the driver is to deliver the correct number of cartons purchased, thereby minimizing any type of suspicion from the buyer.

- **Modus Operandi**: Common tactics include invoice fraud, double brokering, and diversion of cargo through fraudulent means.

- **Impact**: Financial losses, supply chain disruptions, and reputational damage.

Prevention requires vigilant financial controls, thorough background checks, and employee training.

Fictitious Driver Pick-Up

This sophisticated form of Theft involves criminals impersonating legitimate drivers or transport companies to steal cargo.

- **Modus Operandi**: Perpetrators use forged documents and credentials to arrange pick-ups, then disappear with the cargo.

- **Impact**: Significant cargo loss, operational disruptions, financial losses, and loss of trust.

Prevention includes strict verification protocols, technology integration, and employee training.

Warehouse Burglary

Warehouse burglary involves unauthorized entry into storage facilities to steal goods.

- **Modus Operandi**: Detailed surveillance, forced entry or covert access, quick theft operations.

- **Impact**: Financial loss, property damage, supply chain interruptions.

Prevention measures include enhanced physical security, surveillance systems, access control, and employee vigilance.

Tools of the Cargo Thief

Cargo thieves use a range of tools and techniques to carry out their crimes. Understanding these tools helps in developing effective countermeasures.

Physical Tools

- **Bolt Cutters and Crowbars**: Thieves commonly use these

tools to break into containers and vehicles. Bolt cutters can slice through locks and chains, making it easy to access secured areas. Crowbars are used to pry open doors, windows, and containers, allowing quick entry.

- **Lock Picks**: Lock picks are employed to bypass locking mechanisms without damaging them. Skilled thieves can use lock picks to quietly and efficiently unlock doors, gates, and containers, leaving little to no evidence of tampering.

- **Power Tools**: In high-stakes thefts, power tools such as portable drills and saws may be used to quickly cut through metal, wood, or other barriers. These tools can expedite the theft process, allowing thieves to gain access to valuable cargo in minutes.

Technological Tools

- **GPS Jammers**: GPS jammers disrupt tracking devices, making it difficult to locate stolen goods. Thieves can move stolen cargo without being tracked by emitting signals that interfere with GPS trackers, complicating recovery efforts.

- **Hacking Tools**: Hacking tools are utilized to compromise digital security systems. Thieves may hack into logistics networks, tracking systems, or alarm systems to gather information, disable alarms, or reroute shipments. This level of sophistication allows them to execute thefts with minimal risk of detection.

Social Engineering

- **False Identities and Documents**: Thieves often use forged identification and documents to gain access to cargo or information. They can deceive security personnel and gain entry to secure areas by impersonating legitimate drivers, employees, or contractors.

- **Manipulative Tactics**: Social engineering involves convincing employees or security personnel to provide access or information. Thieves may pose as trusted individuals or authority figures, using persuasive tactics to obtain sensitive information or enter restricted areas.

By understanding the tools and techniques used by cargo thieves, security officers can better safeguard against these types of intrusions and protect the cargo.

Freights Targeted by Cargo Thieves

Certain types of freight are particularly attractive to thieves due to their value, demand, and ease of resale.

Electronics: High-value items such as smartphones, laptops, and televisions are easy to resell on the black market. These goods are small and portable and can be quickly sold for cash. For example, a truck transporting a load of new smartphones is an enticing target due to their high resale value and demand.

Pharmaceuticals: Especially high-priced medications or those in high demand, such as painkillers and other prescription drugs. These items are valuable and can be sold illegally. For instance, a shipment of insulin could be targeted because it is expensive and essential for those who need it.

Apparel: Brand-name clothing is easy to move and sell. Items such as designer jeans, sportswear, and luxury fashion goods are often targeted. For example, a truckload of branded sports shoes can be sold quickly through various channels, including online marketplaces and street vendors.

Food and Beverages are often targeted due to their consistent demand and bulk nature. For instance, a truck carrying cases of premium alcohol could be hijacked because the goods are valuable and in high demand, especially during the holiday season.

Understanding the most targeted types of cargo allows security officers to focus their protective efforts more effectively. "Implementing GPS tracking and real-time monitoring can reduce cargo theft incidents by up to 30%[5]," highlighting the importance of using technology to safeguard these high-risk items.

Problems Encountered with Cargo Theft Investigation

Investigating cargo theft poses unique challenges. This section

---

5. CargoNet. (2023). *Implementing GPS tracking and real-time monitoring can reduce cargo theft incidents by up to 30%.:*

explores the common problems faced during these investigations.

Lack of Evidence

Thieves often leave little physical evidence at the scene of a cargo theft. They may use tools and techniques that minimize traces, making it difficult to identify what occurred. For example, lock picks leave fewer marks than a forceful entry with crowbars or bolt cutters.

Delayed Reporting

Cargo theft is sometimes not immediately discovered or reported. Delays can occur due to the time it takes to realize the cargo is missing, leading to a loss of critical time in the investigation. The longer the delay, the more difficult it becomes to recover the stolen goods or identify the perpetrators.

Jurisdictional Issues

Cargo theft often involves multiple jurisdictions, especially when the cargo crosses state or national boundaries. This can complicate the investigation and prosecution process, as different law enforcement agencies may have varying protocols, resources, and legal frameworks.

Insider Involvement

Sometimes, company or logistics chain employees may be involved in the Theft. This insider knowledge can make the investigation sensitive and challenging, as it requires a delicate balance of uncovering the truth without disrupting operations or falsely accusing innocent employees.

Complexity of Supply Chain

The complexity of modern supply chains, with multiple handovers and transit points, can make it difficult to pinpoint where and how the Theft occurred. Each point of transfer introduces potential vulnerabilities, complicating the task of tracking the stolen goods and identifying the culprits.

Technological Challenges

Thieves often use sophisticated methods, including GPS jamming and hacking, to carry out thefts. Staying ahead of these technologies can be a challenge for investigators, requiring constant updates and training in the latest security technologies and tactics.

Understanding these challenges can help security officers and companies develop more effective strategies for preventing cargo theft and aiding in investigations.

What Should Patrol Officers Look For

Patrols play a crucial role in preventing cargo theft. This section outlines what security officers on patrol should look out for.

- **Suspicious Vehicles**: Trucks or vans parked near cargo areas for extended periods without a clear purpose. For instance, a van parked in a loading dock area after business hours could be a red flag.

- **Unusual Activity**: Individuals loitering around cargo areas, especially during odd hours, or showing excessive interest in cargo handling. For example, someone repeatedly walking near a truck yard at night could indicate they are scouting for a potential theft.

- **Improper Identification**: People around cargo areas do not have proper identification or cannot satisfactorily explain their presence. For instance, a person claiming to be a new employee cannot produce any ID or provide details about their role.

- **Tampered Locks or Seals**: Signs that cargo containers, trucks, or storage areas have been tampered with, such as a broken seal on a trailer door or a padlock that looks like it has been cut and replaced.

- **Unsecured Cargo Areas**: Areas where cargo is left unattended or unsecured, making it an easy target for Theft.For instance, pallets of goods are left outside a warehouse without security.

- **Technology Interference**: Evidence of GPS or communication signal disruption can indicate an attempt to interfere with tracking systems. For example, if the GPS signal on a cargo truck suddenly goes offline without explanation, it could suggest tampering.

Vigilant patrols equipped with this knowledge can significantly deter cargo theft incidents.

How Can a Driver Lessen the Chance of Becoming a Cargo Theft Victim

Drivers are often the first line of defense against cargo theft. This section provides tips on how they can minimize the risk.

- **Stay Vigilant**: Be aware of your surroundings, especially at truck stops, rest areas, and during loading/unloading. For instance, a driver should always scan the area for suspicious activity before leaving the vehicle.

- **Secure the Vehicle**: Always lock doors and secure the cargo area, even during shortstops. A driver should never leave the truck unlocked, even if they are only stepping away for a minute.

- **Use Technology**: Employ GPS tracking and keep communication lines open with dispatchers. For example, a driver can use a mobile app to check in with their dispatcher regularly, providing updates on their location and status.

- **Plan Routes Carefully**: Avoid known high-risk areas and vary routes when possible. For instance, a driver might choose an alternate route to avoid a notorious stretch of highway known for cargo thefts.

- **Parking in Secure Areas**: When stopping for rest, choose well-lit, secure parking areas, preferably with surveillance. A driver should avoid isolated rest areas and opt for truck stops with good security measures.

- **Avoid Discussing Cargo**: Do not disclose the nature or value of the cargo to unverified individuals. For example, drivers should avoid discussing their shipment details with strangers at rest stops.

- **Regular Inspection**: Regularly check the integrity of locks, seals, and cargo during transit. For instance, a driver should inspect the trailer and its locks at every stop to ensure nothing has been tampered with.

These proactive measures can significantly reduce the risk of becoming a victim of cargo theft.

Conclusion

As we conclude our exploration of cargo theft and its prevention, it's clear that this issue is not just a concern for individual businesses but a challenge for the global economy. The repercussions of cargo theft extend far beyond the immediate loss of goods; they disrupt supply chains, inflate costs, and undermine the security of global trade.

Throughout this chapter, we have examined various facets of cargo theft, from understanding what constitutes cargo to profiling the typical cargo thief and their methods. We've learned about the tools used in cargo theft and identified the types of freight most commonly targeted. Additionally, we discussed the challenges of investigating cargo theft, the critical role of patrols in prevention, and how drivers can minimize their risk of becoming victims.

Key Takeaways:

- **Vigilance and Awareness**: Awareness and vigilance are the first steps in preventing cargo theft. Security officers, drivers, and all personnel involved in transporting cargo must be constantly alert to the signs of potential Theft.

- **Proactive Measures**: Implementing proactive measures such as strategic route planning, secure parking, use of technology, and thorough background checks can significantly reduce the risk of cargo theft.

- **Collaboration is Key**: Combating cargo theft requires collaboration between various stakeholders, including security personnel, law enforcement, and the transportation industry. Sharing information and best practices is crucial in staying ahead of cargo thieves.

- **Continuous Learning and Adaptation**: As cargo thieves evolve their methods, so must our strategies to combat them. Training and adaptation to new technologies and methods are vital for effective prevention of cargo theft.

- **Community and Network**: Building a trusting network among drivers, security officers, and others in the supply chain can create a community that looks out for one another, making it harder for cargo thieves to operate.

In closing, remember that the fight against cargo theft is ongoing. It requires diligence, intelligence, and a commitment to security at every level. By understanding the nature of cargo theft and applying the strategies outlined in this chapter, security officers can play a pivotal role in safeguarding cargo and maintaining the integrity of the supply chain.

Chapter Eight

Limitations in Use of Force by Security Officers

THE USE OF FORCE is a crucial tool in a security officer's duties, but it comes with significant responsibility and legal considerations. Understanding when and how to appropriately apply force is paramount to not only your safety but also the protection of those you are assigned to safeguard. Imagine you're in a situation where someone's safety is at risk, how do you balance the need to act swiftly with the imperative to use force responsibly?

"Principles of necessity, proportionality, and reasonableness govern the use of force by security officers[1]." This principle underscores the importance of using force only when necessary, applying an

---

1. *The use of force by security officers is governed by principles of necessity, proportionality, and reasonableness.* (2024): https://www.securitystudies.com

amount proportional to the threat, and ensuring that the force used is reasonable. Consider a scenario where a security officer encounters an intruder attempting to break into a restricted area within a corporate office. The intruder is unarmed but refuses to comply with verbal commands to leave. The officer must decide how to proceed. Should they use physical force, or are there other ways to resolve the situation? This decision hinges on the principles of necessity, proportionality, and reasonableness.

Using force is not just about physical action; it's about making split-second decisions with profound implications. Imagine the same officer who, instead of immediately resorting to physical restraint, attempts to de-escalate the situation using verbal communication and authoritative presence. Doing so provides the intruder with an opportunity to comply, thereby reducing the need for physical confrontation.

The importance of using force as a last resort cannot be overstated. Security officers must rely heavily on their training, judgment, and ability to assess situations accurately. Ethical and legal considerations must always guide these decisions, ensuring that actions are justifiable and within the bounds of the law. For instance, if the intruder becomes aggressive and directly threatens the officer or others, the officer might need to use physical restraint. However, this action must be carefully measured and proportionate to the level of threat presented.

In this chapter, we'll discuss the delicate balance between maintaining safety and upholding individuals' rights. We'll explore the importance of thorough training, the application of force as a last resort, and the ethical and legal implications of force application. This foundation will help you understand the gravity of the decision to use force and underscore the importance of training and judgment in such situations.

Training is pivotal in preparing security officers to handle confrontational situations effectively. According to a study published in the International Journal of Security and Safety, proper training in de-escalation techniques can reduce the need for physical force by 40%[2]. This statistic highlights the critical role of continuous training in ensuring that officers are well-equipped to manage conflicts without escalating them unnecessarily.

Furthermore, the application of force is fraught with ethical considerations. The public perception of security officers hinges significantly on how they handle situations involving force. An officer who uses force judiciously and ethically helps maintain the integrity of their profession and fosters trust within the industry they serve.

The legal implications of using force are also profound. Each action a security officer takes is subject to scrutiny under the law. Missteps can lead to legal consequences, not just for the individual officer but also for the employer. Hence, a thorough understanding of legal standards and protocols is indispensable.

---

2. International Journal of Security and Safety. (2023). *Proper training in de-escalation techniques can reduce the need for physical force by 40%*:

By the end of this chapter, you will have a comprehensive understanding of the complexities involved in using force. This knowledge will empower you to make informed decisions that protect both your safety and the rights of those you serve.

Definitions

To navigate the complex landscape of force application effectively, it's essential to understand key terms:

Reasonable Force: This refers to the force necessary to prevent harm or achieve a legitimate security objective without exceeding what is considered appropriate under the circumstances. For instance, if an officer encounters a shoplifter attempting to flee, using a physical hold to detain the individual until law enforcement arrives may be deemed reasonable force.

Excessive Force is the application of force greater than what would be considered necessary or reasonable in a given situation, often leading to legal and ethical violations. Consider a situation where a suspect is already subdued and handcuffed, but an officer continues to use physical force. This is a clear example of excessive force, which could lead to serious legal repercussions and damage to the officer's credibility.

Deadly Force: Any use of force that can reasonably be expected to cause death or serious bodily harm. This includes the use of firearms and other lethal weapons. Imagine a scenario where an officer faces an assailant armed with a knife. If the assailant charges and all other options have been exhausted, the use of a firearm may be justified as deadly forceto protect the officer's life.

Non-Lethal Force: Force that is not likely to cause death or serious bodily harm, such as physical restraints, less-lethal weapons like tasers, and chemical agents like pepper spray. For example, during a public event, officers might use pepper spray to disperse individuals and restore order without causing long-term harm if a crowd becomes unruly.

Understanding these definitions is crucial for security officers to ensure their actions remain within legal and ethical boundaries. Let's consider a real-life example: A security officer at a sports stadium notices a group of individuals becoming increasingly aggressive toward each other. The officer intervenes using verbal commands and positioning to de-escalate the situation. However, when one individual begins physically attacking another, the officer uses a taser to subdue the aggressor. This action demonstrates the appropriate use of non-lethal force—necessary and reasonable to prevent further harm.

It's essential to recognize that each type of force has specific guidelines and training requirements. Officers must be adept at assessing situations and determining the minimal level of force necessary to resolve conflicts. This skill set not only ensures the safety of all involved but also upholds the legal and ethical standards of the security profession.

By understanding and applying these definitions, security officers can confidently and clearly navigate the complex scenarios they face daily. In the following sections, we'll explore the various types of force in detail, discussing their appropriate use, training requirements, and legal implications.

Types of Force

The types of force available to security officers vary, and each comes with its own set of guidelines and considerations:

Constructive Authority

"Constructive authority, through presence and communication, often prevents the need for physical force[3]." This concept involves using presence, communication, and behavior to establish authority and control without physical force.

- **Presence:** A security officer's presence can significantly impact behavior. A professional, confident appearance can convey authority and deter potential threats. For example, a well-dressed officer standing at a building entrance can discourage loitering or unauthorized entry.

- **Verbal Communication:** Clear, concise, and firm communication is key. Effective verbal commands can assert authority and gain compliance. An officer who confidently instructs a crowd to disperse is more likely to achieve

---

3. *Constructive authority, through presence and communication, often prevents the need for physical force.* (2024): https://www.securitystudies.com

compliance than one who hesitates or speaks unclearly.

- **Non-Verbal Cues:** Body language, eye contact, and facial expressions play significant roles. An officer who maintains eye contact and stands upright conveys confidence and authority, which can de-escalate potential conflicts.

Physical Force: This includes manual techniques like holds, restraints, or maneuvers used to control a person. Significant training is required to execute these techniques safely and effectively. For example, a properly applied wrist lock can control a suspect without causing injury.

Mechanical Force: Tools like batons, handcuffs, or restraining devices assist in subduing or controlling individuals. These tools require specific training to be used appropriately and legally.

Chemical Agents: Agents such as pepper spray incapacitate an individual temporarily. Proper use and legal restrictions must be understood to ensure these tools are used appropriately.

Enhanced Mechanical Force

Enhanced mechanical force involves tools or equipment designed to minimize harm while effectively controlling individuals. Proper training and adherence to legal and ethical guidelines are essential.

- **Handcuffs and Restraints:** Used to restrain individuals who pose a threat. It's vital to ensure they are applied securely but not so tightly that they cause injury.

- **Batons:** Used for defense or to gain compliance. The use should be consistent with training and legal guidelines to avoid serious injury.

- **Pepper Spray:** Non-lethal and used to incapacitate temporarily. Proper training focuses on de-escalation and minimizing harm.

- **Tasers:** Deliver temporary electric shocks to incapacitate. Thorough training is necessary to understand when and how to use them appropriately.

Each tool requires specific training and understanding of legal boundaries. Security officers must be trained in the physical use of these tools and decision-making skills to assess when and how to use them appropriately. For instance, research in the International Journal of Security and Safety finds that when properly used, non-lethal weapons significantly reduce the risk of injury to both officers and suspects[4].

Firearms (Deadly Force): Firearm use is considered deadly force and is subject to stringent legal and ethical standards. It is typically reserved for situations where there is an imminent threat to life or serious bodily injury.

---

4. International Journal of Security and Safety. (2023). *Non-lethal weapons, when properly used, significantly reduce the risk of injury to both officers and suspects:*

Self-Defense

Self-defense is a fundamental aspect of a security officer's role, encompassing actions to protect oneself or others from physical harm. However, legal frameworks, ethical considerations, and best practices must guide its application in the field.

Understanding Legal Boundaries

The legal principles governing self-defense vary by jurisdiction but generally allow for reasonable force to protect oneself or others from imminent harm. Security officers must understand the legal boundaries of self-defense in their specific regions. This includes knowing when force is justified, the level of force permissible, and the point at which the threat is considered neutralized.

Principles of Reasonable Force

The concept of reasonable force is central to self-defense. Security officers must assess each situation to determine the minimal level of force necessary to safely resolve it. Excessive force, even in self-defense, can lead to legal consequences and damage to the security organization's reputation. Training in conflict de-escalation is vital to minimize the need for physical force. Proper training in de-escalation techniques can reduce the need for physical forceby 40%.

Training and Preparedness

Effective self-defense requires comprehensive training, including physical skills (like defensive tactics), legal knowledge, and decision-making under stress. Regular training ensures that security officers can confidently handle physical confrontations while remaining within legal and ethical boundaries. Statistics show that 75% of security officers report that regular training updates improve their ability to handle confrontational situations without force.

Defensive Equipment and Tools

Many security officers are equipped with defensive tools, such as batons, pepper spray, or, in some cases, firearms. Strict policies and training should govern the use of these tools. Officers must be adept in using these tools appropriately and understand the specific legal implications of their use.

Documentation and Reporting

Incidents involving self-defense should be meticulously documented and reported. This includes detailed accounts of the incident, the perceived threat, the level of force used, and the outcome. Transparent reporting aids in legal and administrative processes and can be crucial for internal reviews and policy adjustments. Documentation of use-of-force incidents can help mitigate legal repercussions and improve procedural transparency in 60% of cases.

Ethical Considerations and Public Perception

Security officers must balance their right to self-defense with ethical considerations and public perception. The use of force, even when justified, can have significant implications for the relationship between security personnel and the community they serve. Upholding high ethical standards is paramount in maintaining trust and credibility.

Continuous Review and Policy Update

Self-defense policies and training should be dynamic, adapting to new legal rulings, technological advancements, and evolving best practices. Regular reviews of use-of-force incidents can provide valuable insights for training improvements and policy updates.

In summary, self-defense in the context of a security officer's duties is a critical yet complex issue. It requires a careful balance of legal understanding, practical skills, and ethical responsibility. By adhering to the principles of reasonable force, engaging in ongoing training, and upholding transparency and ethical standards, security officers can effectively navigate the challenges of self-defense in their professional roles.

Defense of Others

In security work, the defense of others is a crucial responsibility. Security officers often find themselves in situations where they must act to protect individuals from harm. This duty, however, comes with significant legal and ethical considerations. Officers must ascertain when the use of force is necessary to defend others. The force employed must be reasonable and proportionate to the threat encountered. This means considering non-violent options first and escalating only when necessary.

Imagine a scenario in a busy shopping mall. A security officer notices a man aggressively confronting a woman near the entrance. The situation appears tense, and the woman looks frightened. The officer's first response should be to approach calmly and use verbal commands to de-escalate the situation. "Sir, please step back, and let's talk this through," the officer might say in a firm yet non-threatening tone. Often, a uniform authority figure and the initial verbal intervention can be enough to diffuse tension.

If the aggressor continues to escalate the situation, perhaps by grabbing the woman or making threatening gestures, the officer must quickly assess the threat level. At this point, the officer might employ physical force to separate the individuals, using techniques designed to control them without causing harm. For instance, the officer could use a restraining hold to immobilize the aggressor and protect the victim.

However, if the aggressor shows a weapon or poses an immediate threat to the woman's life, the officer might have to escalate the response further. In this high-risk scenario, the officer could use pepper spray to incapacitate the attacker temporarily, creating a safe space for the woman and preventing further violence. This decision must be guided by the principles of necessity and proportionality, ensuring that the force used is the minimum required to neutralize the threat.

Thorough documentation is essential after the incident. The officer should write a detailed report covering the perceived threat, the rationale behind the decision to use force, and the specifics of the force applied. This report might include statements from witnesses, a timeline of events, and any injuries sustained. Such comprehensive documentation serves multiple purposes: it provides a clear account of events, protects the officer and their employer from potential legal consequences, and aids in internal reviews to refine future training and policies.

Moreover, transparent documentation helps build trust within the community, as it demonstrates a commitment to accountability and ethical conduct. It also ensures that any use-of-force incident can withstand legal scrutiny, which is crucial in maintaining the integrity of the security profession.

Warning Shots

The use of warning shots by security officers is a contentious issue. Warning shots are firearm discharges intended to signal a stop or deter an aggressor. However, due to their potential risks, many jurisdictions discourage or even prohibit their use. The unpredictability of where a bullet will end up can lead to unintended harm, property damage, or legal complications.

For these reasons, security officers are generally advised to seek alternative de-escalation methods. Verbal warnings, physical presence, and non-lethal tools should be the first line of response. If a situation escalates, officers must carefully assess the need for force, remembering that every discharged bullet carries significant legal and ethical weight.

Consider a situation at a large outdoor event. A security officer spots a group of individuals becoming increasingly aggressive towards one another. Instead of resorting to a warning shot to disperse the group, the officer could use a loud, authoritative verbal command. "Everyone, step back now and disperse," the officer might shout, projecting confidence and control.

If the verbal command is ignored and the confrontation escalates, the officer could then consider using non-lethal options. For example, deploying a taser to incapacitate the most aggressive individual can halt the altercation without the risks associated with firing a warning shot. This approach ensures that the officer addresses the threat effectively while minimizing the potential for collateral damage.

The decision to avoid warning shots aligns with the broader principle that every action taken by a security officer must be justified as necessary and proportionate. By prioritizing verbal commands and non-lethal options, officers can manage threats effectively while upholding the highest standards of safety and responsibility.

Furthermore, when an officer decides against using a warning shot, it reflects a deep understanding of the legal and ethical implications involved. Each situation is unique, and officers must be adept at reading the dynamics of conflict, choosing responses that protect lives and property without unnecessary escalation.

Defense of Premises or Personal Property

Defending property is a key aspect of a security officer's role. However, the legal boundaries surrounding using force to protect property are generally more restrictive than those for self-defense or the defense of others. It is necessary to adhere to your state and local jurisdiction policies on the limitation of the use of force by security officers. Officers must assess each situation carefully to determine whether the use of force is justified. In many cases, non-violent methods such as enhanced surveillance, locks, and alarms are more appropriate.

For example, a security officer patrolling a corporate office complex at night notices an individual attempting to enter a secured storage room. The officer's first action should be issuing a clear warning: "Stop right there! This area is off-limits!" Such a command can often deter the would-be intruder and prevent the need for physical intervention.

If the intruder ignores the warning and attempts to force entry, the officer might consider using physical restraint and contacting law enforcement officers immediately. Suppose the officer approaches and uses a secure wrist lock to control the intruder without causing harm. This method of physical restraint is proportionate to the threat posed and aims to neutralize the situation without unnecessary violence.

When verbal and physical interventions are insufficient, the officer might need to employ handcuffs to detain the intruder until law enforcement arrives. This escalation should be based on the principle of proportionality, ensuring that the force used is appropriate to the threat level.

Comprehensive documentation of these incidents is critical. The officer should record details about the perceived threat, the actions taken in response, and any aftermath, including the condition of the intruder and any property damage. This documentation provides a clear account of events and protects the officer and their employer in legal proceedings.

Moreover, thorough reporting aids in internal reviews, helping organizations refine their security protocols and training programs. For instance, if a pattern of break-ins is identified, the organization might invest in additional security measures, such as improved lighting, advanced alarm systems, or increased patrols during vulnerable hours.

Security officers must understand and respect the legal boundaries of defending property. By employing non-deadly methods first and escalating only when necessary, officers can effectively protect property while minimizing the risk of legal repercussions and maintaining the highest ethical standards.

In summary, the defense of premises or personal property involves a careful balance of deterrence, appropriate use of force, and comprehensive documentation. Security officers must be prepared to respond to threats swiftly and proportionately, always prioritizing non-violent methods whenever possible. Through proper training and adherence to legal and ethical guidelines, officers can safeguard property while upholding the integrity of their profession.

Scope of Liability

Liability in the use of force is a critical concern for security officers.

Both civil and criminal liabilities can arise from instances where force is used. Factors influencing liability include the reasonableness of the force, adherence to legal standards and protocols, and the outcomes of the action.

Imagine a situation where a security officer at a large sporting event intervenes in a physical altercation between fans. In the heat of the moment, the officer uses a baton to subdue one of the individuals involved. If this action results in injury, the officer could face civil litigation from the injured party and potential criminal charges if the force is deemed excessive or unjustified.

To mitigate such risks, security officers must operate within the bounds of established legal and procedural guidelines. The concept of "reasonableness" is pivotal here. The force used must be proportionate to the threat faced. If an unarmed individual is simply being unruly, the use of a baton might be considered excessive. However, the same action might be deemed reasonable if the individual poses an immediate threat to others' safety.

Minimizing liability risks involves regular training, strict adherence to legal and procedural guidelines, and comprehensive documentation of all force-related incidents. Training programs should cover physical tactics and the legal ramifications of using force. For instance, role-playing scenarios can help officers practice decision-making under pressure, ensuring they can act swiftly and appropriately in real situations.

Comprehensive documentation is another critical component. Every use-of-force incident should be meticulously recorded, including the context of the incident, the perceived threat, the force used, and the outcome. This documentation serves multiple purposes: it provides a clear account for internal reviews, aids in legal defenses, and ensures transparency. According to statistics, documentation of use-of-force incidents can help in 60% of cases to mitigate legal repercussions and improve procedural transparency.

Case studies of real-life incidents where liability issues arose can provide valuable lessons. For example, a study published in the American Journal of Criminal Justice reports that comprehensive use-of-force policies and regular audits can decrease incidents of excessive force by 25%[5]. Security officers can learn how to navigate complex situations and avoid common pitfalls by analyzing past cases.

Consider a case where a security officer at a nightclub used pepper spray to break up a fight. The subsequent legal proceedings revealed that the officer had not followed proper protocol for its use, leading to significant liability for both the officer and the employing security firm. Had the officer adhered to the established guidelines and documented the incident thoroughly, the outcome could have been different.

Regular audits of use-of-force incidents help ensure policy compliance and identify improvement areas. These audits should be

---

5. American Journal of Criminal Justice. (2023). *Comprehensive use-of-force policies and regular audits can decrease incidents of excessive force by 25%:*

conducted impartially and cover all aspects of the incident, from the initial threat assessment to the final resolution. Feedback from these audits can be used to refine training programs and update protocols, fostering a culture of continuous improvement.

As we conclude this chapter on the use of force, it's imperative to reflect on the critical responsibilities that come with the role of a security officer. The decision to use force is not one to be taken lightly. It carries significant legal, ethical, and moral weight. This chapter has explored the various aspects of using force, from understanding the foundational principles and definitions to examining specific applications like the defense of others, warning shots, and the protection of property.

Key takeaways from this chapter include:

Judicious Use of Force: The foremost lesson is the need for judicious and responsible use of force. Security officers must always assess situations carefully, using force only when necessary and in a manner that is proportional to the threat.

Training and Knowledge: Continuous training and knowledge are essential in making informed decisions about using force. This includes understanding the legal ramifications, mastering de-escalation techniques, and proficiently using tools and equipment.

Constructive Authority: This chapter emphasizes the power of constructive authority and highlights the importance of presence, verbal communication, and nonverbal cues in managing situations effectively without resorting to physical force.

Ethical and Legal Considerations: Security officers must always be cognizant of the ethical and legal frameworks governing the use of force. Adherence to these guidelines protects the officer and upholds the integrity of the security profession.

Documentation and Accountability: Proper documentation and accountability are crucial in instances where force is used. This ensures transparency and provides a necessary record for legal and administrative purposes.

Community and Empathy: Finally, the role of empathy and understanding in security work cannot be understated. Building a rapport with the community and understanding the nuances of human behavior can often preempt the need for force.

In conclusion, using force is a complex aspect of security work that demands careful consideration and constant evaluation. Security officers must balance the need to protect with the duty to respect individuals' rights and dignity. By following the guidelines and principles outlined in this chapter, officers can ensure that their actions are justified, responsible, and in accordance with the highest standards of the security profession.

Chapter Nine

Incident Command System – Emergency Response

EFFECTIVE RESOURCE MANAGEMENT AND coordination are vital in the high-stakes arena of emergency response. The Incident Command System (ICS) is a cornerstone in this domain, offering a structured approach to handling emergencies of all types and scales. This chapter introduces ICS, underscoring its importance in ensuring efficient, coordinated responses to incidents ranging from natural disasters to security breaches.

ICS is a versatile, widely adopted framework for managing emergencies. It provides a standardized yet flexible structure, enabling different agencies and personnel to work together harmoniously. Understanding ICS is essential for security officers and emergency responders, as it forms the backbone of organized, effective crisis management.

Imagine multiple agencies responding to a massive wildfire

threatening a community. Without a coordinated approach, efforts could be duplicated, resources wasted, and critical information lost. ICS prevents such chaos by establishing clear roles and procedures, ensuring that every action is purposeful and efficient. This system is about managing resources and safeguarding lives and property through meticulous planning and execution.

In the chaos of an emergency, the stakes are incredibly high. Lives, property, and the environment hang in the balance. This is where the Incident Command System (ICS) comes into play, providing the structure and coordination needed to manage such critical situations effectively. ICS isn't just a tool; it's the backbone of organized, efficient emergency response, ensuring that all actions are directed towards a common goal: mitigating the impact of the incident as swiftly and safely as possible.

The ICS framework establishes a clear hierarchy, ensuring everyone knows their role and responsibilities, which is crucial for maintaining order and efficiency in chaotic situations.

Training is at the heart of effective ICS implementation. Security officers and emergency responders must be well-versed in ICS principles and procedures. Regular training exercises help ensure everyone involved in an emergency response is familiar with the system and can operate effectively. This preparation is crucial, as it allows for a seamless transition from routine operations to emergency response, ensuring that resources are deployed quickly and efficiently when needed.

As we explore this chapter in depth, we will explore the components and functions of ICS, its history, its benefits, and how it is applied in various emergency scenarios. This theoretical and practical knowledge provides the foundation for effective, coordinated action in the face of crises. The goal is to equip you with the understanding and skills to navigate complex emergencies confidently and competently, ensuring that every response is as effective and efficient as possible.

What is ICS?

The Incident Command System (ICS) is a systematic tool designed to command, control, and coordinate emergency response efforts. It is widely recognized for providing a standardized, nationwide approach to managing incidents, ensuring that all responding agencies and personnel can work together effectively, regardless of the scale or nature of the emergency.

Standardized Organizational Structure

ICS is meticulously organized into five primary functions, each with specific roles and responsibilities, ensuring a comprehensive response to any incident.

Scalability and Flexibility

One of ICS's greatest strengths is its scalability and flexibility. The system is designed to expand or contract based on the needs of the incident, making it applicable to a wide range of situations, from small local emergencies to large-scale disasters involving multiple jurisdictions. This adaptability allows ICS to be tailored to fit the specific demands of any incident, ensuring an effective and efficient response.

For example, during a minor chemical spill in a small community, a simplified ICS structure might involve just a few key personnel managing the response. Conversely, in the aftermath of a major hurricane impacting several states, a full-scale ICS structure involving federal, state, and local agencies would be implemented. This flexibility ensures that ICS can provide the appropriate level of organization and coordination for any scenario.

Unified Command Structure

ICS supports a unified command approach in multi-agency responses, where agencies collaborate and share responsibilities. This unified command structure ensures that all participating agencies have a voice in decision-making and that their resources are used efficiently. It fosters teamwork and minimizes confusion, ensuring all actions are aligned with the overall incident objectives.

"Effective communication and clear command structures are the cornerstones of successful incident management[1]." This quote encapsulates the essence of ICS, highlighting the importance of structured communication and leadership in crises. By establishing

---

1. *Effective communication and clear command structures are the cornerstones of successful incident management.* (2024): https://www.emergencyresponse.com

a common language and structure, ICS ensures that all responders communicate effectively and work towards a common goal.

For instance, ICS enables federal, state, and local agencies to work seamlessly during a major hurricane response. It allows for coordinated efforts in resource allocation, search and rescue operations, and aid delivery, ensuring that assistance reaches affected areas promptly and effectively. The result is a unified, efficient response that maximizes resource utilization and minimizes redundancy and confusion.

History of Incident Command System

The Incident Command System (ICS) was developed in response to a critical need for better coordination during complex incidents. Its origins trace back to the 1970s, following a series of catastrophic wildfires in Southern California. These devastating fires highlighted significant inter-agency coordination and resource management challenges, prompting the re-evaluating of emergency response strategies.

FIRESCOPE: The Birth of ICS

The FIRESCOPE (Firefighting Resources of California Organized for Potential Emergencies) program was initiated to address these challenges. This program aimed to create a system that could unify various firefighting agencies and resources under a common structure. The development of ICS under FIRESCOPE marked a revolutionary shift in emergency management, introducing a standardized, flexible framework that could be scaled to meet the needs of any incident.

ICS proved its effectiveness in managing wildfires, demonstrating significant coordination and resource utilization improvements. This success led to its adoption beyond firefighting, as other emergency response disciplines recognized the benefits of a standardized command system. ICS was subsequently integrated into the broader framework of the National Incident Management System (NIMS), providing a consistent nationwide template for incident management.

National Adoption and Evolution

Today, ICS is integral to the National Emergency Management System (NIMS), enabling all government, private-sector, and non-governmental organizations to work together during incidents. Its adoption as a national standard underscores its effectiveness in managing a wide range of emergencies, from natural disasters to security incidents.

A poignant example of ICS's effectiveness is its use during the 9/11 attacks. The coordinated efforts among numerous agencies, facilitated by ICS, significantly enhanced the overall response efficiency. The ability to quickly establish a unified command structure, integrate resources, and implement a coordinated strategy was critical in managing the response to one of the most challenging incidents in modern history.

Research published in the International Journal of Disaster Risk

Reduction demonstrates how ICS improves resource management and operational efficiency during crises[2]. Additionally, an analysis in the Homeland Security Affairs journal emphasizes the role of ICS in enhancing interagency communication and cooperation, further validating its effectiveness as a critical tool in emergency management[3].

In summary, the development and evolution of ICS reflect a continual commitment to improving emergency response. Its standardized approach, scalability, and emphasis on clear communication and collaboration make it an indispensable framework for managing incidents of all types and scales. For security officers and emergency responders, mastering ICS is essential for effective, coordinated action in crises.

Benefits of ICS

Implementing the Incident Command System (ICS) offers numerous advantages in emergency management, making it an indispensable framework for effectively responding to crises. Let's explore the specific benefits that ICS brings to the table:

---

2. International Journal of Disaster Risk Reduction. (2023). *ICS improves resource management and operational efficiency during crises:*

3. Homeland Security Affairs. (2023). *ICS enhances interagency communication and cooperation:* https://www.hsa.org

Enhanced Interagency Coordination

One of the standout advantages of ICS is its ability to enhance interagency coordination. ICS facilitates seamless cooperation among different agencies by providing a common structure, which is crucial in large-scale or complex incidents. Imagine a scenario involving a major earthquake where federal, state, and local agencies and non-governmental organizations must work together. Without ICS, the lack of coordination could lead to duplicated efforts, miscommunication, and inefficient resource utilization. With ICS, however, each agency understands its role and responsibilities, fostering a collaborative environment that streamlines response efforts.

Effective Resource Management

ICS ensures the efficient utilization and allocation of resources, avoiding duplication of efforts and minimizing response times. Statistics show that ICS implementation has been credited with a 25% increase in the efficiency of resource allocation during disasters[4]. This efficiency is vital when every second counts, such as in the aftermath of a hurricane, where timely distribution of food, water, and medical supplies can save lives. ICS's structured approach to resource management ensures that available assets are used where

---

4. FEMA. (2023). *ICS implementation has been credited with a 25% increase in the efficiency of resource allocation during disasters*:

they are needed most, maximizing the impact of the response.

Clear Communication

The standardized format of ICS promotes clear, concise communication, reducing confusion and misunderstandings during emergencies. Training programs in ICS protocols have led to a 40% reduction in miscommunication during multi-agency responses[5]. Clear communication is the backbone of effective emergency management. For instance, during a wildfire, ICS enables fire departments, emergency medical services, and law enforcement to share information and coordinate their actions seamlessly, ensuring that efforts are synchronized and objectives are met efficiently.

Accountability and Documentation

ICS encourages detailed record-keeping and accountability, aiding post-incident evaluation and continuous improvement of emergency response strategies. Comprehensive documentation of actions, decisions, and resource utilization helps understand what worked well and what areas need improvement. This accountability is crucial for refining future responses and ensuring that lessons learned are integrated into standard operating procedures.

---

5. FEMA. (2023). *Training programs in ICS protocols have led to a 40% reduction in miscommunication during multi-agency responses*:

Real-World Effectiveness

Case studies of incidents where ICS was effectively deployed, such as during Hurricane Katrina and the COVID-19 pandemic, demonstrate its effectiveness in diverse scenarios. For example, during Hurricane Katrina, ICS facilitated the coordination of multiple federal and state agencies, enabling a more organized and effective response to one of the most devastating natural disasters in U.S. history. Similarly, during the COVID-19 pandemic, ICS was instrumental in managing the distribution of medical supplies and vaccines, demonstrating its adaptability to various emergencies.

Research published in the International Journal of Disaster Risk Reduction underscores how ICS improves resource management and operational efficiency during crises. Furthermore, an analysis in the Homeland Security Affairs journal highlights the role of ICS in enhancing interagency communication and cooperation, further validating its effectiveness as a critical tool in emergency management[6].

In summary, ICS has manifold benefits, from enhancing coordination and communication to ensuring efficient resource management and accountability. Its structured approach and flexibility make it a cornerstone of effective emergency response, capable of adapting to the unique challenges presented by different crises.

---

6. Homeland Security Affairs. (2023). *ICS enhances interagency communication and cooperation:* https://www.hsa.org

Basic Features of ICS

The Incident Command System (ICS) is characterized by several fundamental features that contribute to its effectiveness in managing emergencies. These features ensure that ICS can adapt to the needs of any incident, providing a structured yet flexible approach to crisis management.

Standardization

ICS employs standardized terminology and procedures, ensuring clear understanding and consistency in multi-agency responses. This standardization eliminates ambiguity and ensures that all responders can communicate effectively, regardless of agency or background. For instance, standardized terms for incident status, resource needs, and operational objectives prevent misinterpretations that could hinder response efforts.

Modular Organization

The structure of ICS is modular, allowing it to expand or contract based on the needs of the incident. This flexibility is crucial for scaling the response to match the incident's complexity and demands. ICS starts small, with a basic command structure, and can grow to accommodate more functions and personnel as the situation evolves. This modularity was notably effective during the Deepwater Horizon oil spill. ICS facilitated the coordination of multiple federal and state agencies, private sector partners, and non-governmental organizations, adapting as the response efforts expanded.

Management by Objectives

ICS operates through clearly defined objectives, which the Incident Commander determines. These objectives drive operational activities and resource allocation, ensuring that every action taken aligns with the overall goals of the response. This approach helps maintain focus and direction, preventing resources from being wasted on non-essential tasks.

Integrated Communications

ICS prioritizes an integrated communications plan with common communication protocols, ensuring that all personnel can communicate effectively across various agencies. Integrated communications prevent information silos and ensure that everyone involved in the response is on the same page. During the 2017 hurricanes, for example, integrated communications facilitated the coordination of search and rescue operations, medical response, and aid distribution across multiple states.

Unity of Command and Chain of Command

Unity of command ensures that every individual has a designated supervisor, establishing a clear line of authority. The chain of command helps streamline decisions and requests, preventing confusion and ensuring that commands are followed efficiently. This principle ensures that instructions flow smoothly from the Incident Commander to all responders, maintaining order and discipline during chaotic situations.

Unified Command

In situations involving multiple agencies, a unified command ensures joint decision-making and resource allocation, fostering collaboration. This approach allows agencies with different jurisdictions and expertise to work together effectively, ensuring that the response is cohesive and comprehensive. For instance, during a large-scale terrorist attack, unified command enables law enforcement, emergency medical services, and federal agencies to coordinate their efforts seamlessly, enhancing the overall effectiveness of the response.

Comprehensive Resource Management

ICS includes processes for categorizing, ordering, dispatching, tracking, and recovering resources. It ensures efficient use and turnaround of resources, preventing shortages and bottlenecks. This comprehensive approach to resource management was crucial during the response to the Deepwater Horizon oil spill, where vast amounts of equipment, personnel, and supplies needed to be managed and deployed effectively.

The basic features of ICS – standardization, modular organization, management by objectives, integrated communications, unity of command, unified command, and comprehensive resource management – form the foundation of a robust and adaptable emergency management system. These features enable ICS to provide clear guidelines and roles for responders, ensuring that every action is purposeful, efficient, and coordinated.

Incident Command and Command Staff Functions

The Incident Command and Command Staff are the backbone of the ICS structure, ensuring that every aspect of the emergency response is managed efficiently and effectively. These roles are designed to facilitate clear communication, maintain safety, and foster cooperation among all involved agencies and personnel.

Incident Commander

The Incident Commander (IC) is at the helm of the response operation and is responsible for all aspects of incident management. This role involves developing strategic objectives, making high-stakes decisions, and ensuring that all operations align with the overall response goals. The IC must possess strong leadership qualities, a clear vision, and the ability to make quick, informed decisions under pressure. They lead both the command and general staff, ensuring that every action taken is purposeful and coordinated.

Imagine the response to a large-scale natural disaster like Hurricane Katrina. The Incident Commander would make critical decisions about evacuation routes, resource allocation, and coordination with federal and state agencies. Their leadership would guide the entire operation to minimize harm and expedite recovery efforts.

Public Information Officer

The Public Information Officer (PIO) is responsible for managing public communications and media relations and disseminating information about the incident. This role is crucial for maintaining public trust and ensuring accurate, timely information reaches the community and media outlets. The PIO coordinates with other agencies to provide a unified message, helping to prevent misinformation and panic.

During the Boston Marathon bombing response, the PIO was vital in informing the public about safety measures, ongoing investigations, and recovery efforts. Their clear and consistent communication helped to reassure the public and provide necessary updates.

Safety Officer

The Safety Officer (SO) identifies and mitigates health and safety hazards, ensuring the safety and well-being of all responders. This role involves conducting risk assessments, implementing safety protocols, and continuously monitoring conditions to prevent accidents and injuries. The SO's vigilance is critical in high-risk environments, such as chemical spills or large-scale natural disasters, where the potential for harm is significant.

For example, in a hazardous material spill, the Safety Officer would be responsible for ensuring that all responders have the appropriate protective gear, are aware of the risks, and follow safety procedures to prevent exposure and injuries.

Liaison Officer

The Liaison Officer (LO) is the primary contact for supporting agencies, ensuring cooperation and communication among all involved parties. This role is essential for coordinating efforts across different organizations, facilitating resource sharing, and addressing any interagency issues that arise. The LO helps to integrate the efforts of various agencies into a cohesive response strategy.

During the response to the Boston Marathon bombing, the Liaison Officer coordinated efforts between local police, federal agencies, emergency medical services, and other support organizations, ensuring that all entities worked together seamlessly to manage the crisis.

An example of these roles in action can be seen during the Boston Marathon bombing response, where the unified command structure and designated roles ensured a coordinated and effective response.

General Staff Functions

The General Staff in ICS handles the tactical aspects of the incident response, managing the on-the-ground operations crucial for achieving the incident objectives. Each section has specific responsibilities, ensuring a comprehensive and effective response.

Operations Section

The Operations Section manages tactical operations to achieve the incident objectives. This includes directing all resources and task forces to ensure that the strategic goals set by the Incident Commander are met. The Operations Section Chief must thoroughly understand the incident's dynamics and be capable of making real-time decisions to adapt to changing conditions.

Consider the extensive wildfires in California. The Operations Section would coordinate the deployment of firefighting teams, manage evacuation procedures, and ensure that fire suppression efforts are effectively carried out, prioritizing areas based on threat levels and resource availability.

Planning Section

The Planning Section collects, evaluates, and disseminates operational information. This section develops the Incident Action Plan (IAP), which outlines the objectives and strategies for the response. The Planning Section ensures that all information is up-to-date and adjusts plans as new information becomes available.

During a major flood, the Planning Section would gather data on water levels, weather forecasts, and affected areas to create an IAP that guides rescue and relief operations. This planning ensures that resources are allocated where needed and that all responders know the operational priorities.

Logistics Section

The Logistics Section provides the necessary resources, services, and support to meet operational needs, including transportation, supplies, and facilities. This section ensures that responders have everything they need to perform their tasks effectively, from food and medical supplies to vehicles and communication equipment.

In the aftermath of a hurricane, the Logistics Section would be responsible for setting up emergency shelters, coordinating the delivery of relief supplies, and ensuring that all response teams' logistical needs are met promptly and efficiently.

Finance or Administration Section

The Finance/Administration Section manages the incident's financial, administrative, and cost analysis aspects. This includes tracking expenditures, managing contracts, and ensuring that all financial operations are transparent and accountable. The section ensures that funds are used appropriately and that all financial records are meticulously maintained.

During the California wildfires, the efficient coordination of these sections under ICS was pivotal in managing resources, supporting firefighters, and ensuring financial oversight. The Finance/Administration Section tracked expenses related to firefighting efforts, ensuring that resources were used effectively and that the response was financially sustainable.

In conclusion, the Incident Commander and General Staff functions are integral to effectively managing emergencies. By clearly defining roles and responsibilities, ICS ensures that every aspect of the response is handled efficiently, from strategic decision-making to on-the-ground operations. This structured approach enhances coordination and communication and ensures that resources are used effectively and that the response is safe and accountable.

Common Responsibilities

Certain responsibilities are common across all ICS roles, forming the bedrock of effective incident management. These shared duties ensure that every team member contributes to a coordinated and efficient response regardless of their specific function.

Understanding and Implementing ICS

Every personnel involved in an incident response must have a solid understanding of ICS principles and functions. This knowledge is the foundation upon which all other activities are built. Familiarity with the ICS structure, roles, and procedures allows each team member to perform their duties effectively and ensures seamless integration into the overall response effort. Regular training and drills are essential to maintain this level of readiness and understanding.

Effective Communication

Clear and concise communication is vital for the successful flow of information and the execution of tasks. In high-pressure emergencies, miscommunication can lead to critical delays or errors. Utilizing standardized terminology and communication protocols within ICS ensures that all team members understand each other, reducing the risk of misunderstandings. Effective communication also extends to public information dissemination, where accurate updates prevent panic and provide reassurance.

Safety First

Ensuring the safety of personnel and the public is a top priority. This principle guides every decision and action within ICS. Safety officers are critical in identifying potential hazards and implementing measures to mitigate them. However, safety is a shared responsibility, and every team member must remain vigilant and adhere to established safety protocols. Prioritizing safety protects lives and maintains the integrity and effectiveness of the response effort.

Resource Tracking

Efficient resource monitoring and management are crucial for effective incident management. This includes tracking personnel, equipment, and supplies to ensure they are available when and where needed. Resource tracking helps prevent duplication, waste, and shortages, ensuring that the response remains efficient and effective. Advanced tracking systems and real-time updates facilitate better coordination and decision-making.

Documentation

Maintaining accurate and comprehensive records of actions, decisions, and communications is crucial for accountability and future reference. Proper documentation serves multiple purposes: it provides a clear record of events, supports legal and administrative processes, and offers valuable insights for post-incident reviews. Statistics show that proper documentation of use-of-force incidents can help mitigate legal repercussions and improve procedural transparency in 60% of cases. Thorough documentation also aids in refining policies and training programs, contributing to continuous improvement.

Conclusion

As we conclude our exploration of the Incident Command System (ICS), it's clear that ICS is not just a framework but a crucial philosophy in emergency management. Its structured approach and adaptability make it an indispensable tool in various emergency scenarios, from natural disasters to security incidents. ICS's strengths lie in its standardized procedures, clear command structure, and emphasis on unified collaboration and communication.

The modular organization of ICS, expanding or contracting based on incident needs, allows for flexible and scalable responses. Its management by objectives ensures that every action taken is goal-oriented and efficient. The integrated communication system prevents information silos and ensures that all participants are on the same page.

Key roles within ICS, such as the Incident Commander, Command Staff, and General Staff, each have distinct but complementary functions, ensuring a comprehensive response to any incident. The unified command structure is particularly valuable in multi-agency or multi-jurisdictional incidents, fostering cooperation and preventing conflicts.

The common responsibilities across all ICS roles – including understanding the system, clear communication, prioritizing safety, efficient resource tracking, and thorough documentation – are foundational principles that transcend specific incidents. They represent best practices in emergency management and are applicable in a broad spectrum of situations.

The Incident Command System embodies a collaborative, systematic, and efficient approach to managing emergencies. For security officers and emergency responders, a deep understanding of ICS is beneficial and essential for effective and responsible incident management. As challenges in emergency response continue to evolve, so will ICS's strategies and applications, reinforcing its status as a dynamic and enduring tool in emergency and crisis management.

Key Takeaways

1. **Structured Coordination**: ICS provides a clear, structured framework that enhances coordination among various agencies and personnel, ensuring a unified response to emergencies.

2. **Effective Resource Management**: The system's resource allocation and tracking efficiency significantly improve operational effectiveness during crises.

3. **Clear Communication**: Standardized communication protocols within ICS reduce miscommunication and ensure that information flows smoothly among all parties involved.

4. **Safety Prioritization**: The emphasis on safety within ICS ensures that responders and the public are protected,

guiding all operational decisions.

5. **Accountability and Improvement**: Comprehensive documentation within ICS aids in accountability, legal processes, and continuous improvement through post-incident analysis.

6. **Adaptability and Scalability**: ICS's modular nature allows it to scale according to the incident's complexity, making it versatile for various emergencies.

7. **Unified Command**: In multi-agency incidents, the unified command structure within ICS fosters collaboration, prevents conflicts, and enhances the overall response.

By internalizing these principles and continuously honing their skills within the ICS framework, security officers and emergency responders can ensure that their actions are efficient, effective, and aligned with the highest emergency management standards.

Chapter Ten

Document Fraud

IMAGINE FACING A SCENARIO where a single forged document threatens the integrity of an entire organization. Document fraud is not just about falsified papers; it's about the potential chaos they can unleash. Document fraud is a formidable challenge in today's security landscape, from individual identity theft to national security breaches. It involves the falsification or unauthorized creation of official documents, leveraging advanced technology to amplify its prevalence. How do we combat this growing menace?

"Effective communication and clear command structures are the cornerstones of successful incident management." Similarly, addressing document fraud requires a nuanced approach, balancing vigilance with expertise. Document fraud can take many forms: altering legitimate documents, manufacturing counterfeit ones, or misusing legitimate documents for fraud. The implications are vast, impacting individuals, institutions, and public safety.

As security professionals, our role in preventing document fraud is critical. We are the gatekeepers who ensure that the documents being used are legitimate and that the people presenting them are who they claim to be. This responsibility requires a keen eye for detail and a deep understanding of the various methods used by fraudsters and the tools available to detect and prevent such fraud.

Imagine the repercussions of a forged passport enabling a dangerous individual to cross borders undetected or a counterfeit diploma allowing an unqualified person to practice medicine. The stakes are incredibly high. Security professionals must have the knowledge and skills to effectively recognize and address document fraud. Are you ready to tackle this head-on?

The Importance of Security's Role in Preventing Document Fraud

Preventing document fraud is not just about protecting the immediate interests of an organization; it's about safeguarding the broader community and national security. Here's why our role is so crucial:

1. **Protection of Identity and Personal Information:** Identity theft can devastate individuals, leading to financial loss, legal issues, and emotional distress. By preventing document fraud, security professionals protect individuals from such personal catastrophes.

2. **Maintaining Organizational Integrity:** A single fraudulent document can compromise the integrity of an entire organization. The repercussions can be severe, whether it's a fake employee badge that grants unauthorized access to sensitive areas or forged financial documents that

lead to financial loss.

3. **Enhancing National Security:** Forged documents such as passports and visas can pose significant threats to national security on a larger scale. Preventing these forgeries helps prevent potentially dangerous individuals from entering the country or engaging in illegal activities.

4. **Supporting Legal Compliance:** Many industries have strict regulations regarding document verification. Ensuring that documents are legitimate helps organizations comply with these laws, avoiding hefty fines and legal repercussions.

5. **Facilitating Trust and Credibility:** In fields like banking, healthcare, and education, document authenticity underpins the trust of clients and the public place in these institutions. Effective document fraud prevention helps maintain this trust.

Statistics show that document fraud accounts for over $650 billion in global financial losses annually[1]. This staggering figure underscores the critical need for robust fraud prevention measures. Every forged document represents a potential financial loss and a breach of trust and security.

As we delve deeper into the specifics of document fraud, it's

---

1. Association of Certified Fraud Examiners. (2023). *Document fraud accounts for over $650 billion in global financial losses annually*:

important to remember the broader implications of our work. The tools and techniques we use to detect and prevent fraud are not just technical skills; they are vital components of a larger mission to protect individuals, maintain organizational integrity, and ensure public safety.

Understanding the various forms of document fraud, staying updated on the latest detection technologies, and continuously improving your vigilance are essential steps in this ongoing battle.

Security Features

Understanding the security features embedded within genuine documents is crucial in the battle against document fraud. These features are meticulously designed to deter forgery and unauthorized duplication. Imagine the complexity behind a simple passport—it's not just a piece of paper but a fortress of security measures working in unison to verify authenticity. Let's explore the key features that make a document genuine and secure.

Holograms

Holograms provide a visual security element that is incredibly difficult to replicate. These intricate, three-dimensional images change when viewed from different angles, offering a dynamic layer of authentication. When you tilt a passport or driver's license, the hologram might display various patterns or images, making it nearly impossible for forgers to create a convincing duplicate. This dynamic security feature acts as a quick and effective visual check.

Watermarks

Watermarks are subtle images or patterns that become visible when the document is held up to light. Watermarks are an effective authentication tool that is seamlessly integrated into the document's design. They are often used in official documents like banknotes, passports, and birth certificates. The presence of a genuine watermark can be a clear indicator of authenticity, adding a layer of security that is challenging to forge.

Microprinting

Microprinting involves tiny, detailed text or patterns that are difficult to reproduce without specialized printing technology. This security feature might appear as a thin line or pattern to the naked eye, but it reveals detailed text or intricate designs under magnification. Microprinting is commonly found on banknotes and legal documents, providing a small but significant hurdle for counterfeiters. Its precision makes it a robust security measure.

Color-Shifting Ink

Color-shifting ink changes color depending on the viewing angle, adding another layer of complexity to forgery attempts. This feature is often used on currency and high-security documents to ensure they are not easily replicated. For example, a color-shifting element might change from green to gold on a legitimate driver's license as you tilt it. This dynamic feature requires advanced printing techniques and is highly effective in deterring fraud.

Biometric Data

Incorporating biometric data, such as fingerprints or facial recognition information, links the document unmistakably to its rightful owner. This advanced security feature significantly enhances the document's authenticity. Biometric data is becoming increasingly common in passports and national ID cards, providing a level of security unique to the individual holder. Unlike other features that can be mimicked, biometric data offers a personalized layer of protection that is extremely hard to forge.

The Importance of Security Features

A study published in the Journal of Financial Crime highlighted that businesses investing in advanced document verification technologies saw a 40% reduction in fraud attempts[2]. This demonstrates the critical importance of integrating sophisticated security features into documents to combat fraud effectively. These features help verify the authenticity of documents and serve as powerful deterrents against those attempting to commit fraud.

Consider a high-security event requiring identity verification for entry. Security personnel must quickly and accurately verify the authenticity of attendees' identification documents. Security

---

2. Journal of Financial Crime. (2023). *Businesses investing in advanced document verification technologies saw a 40% reduction in fraud attempts:*

officers can confidently determine whether a document is genuine by examining holograms, watermarks, microprinting, and color-shifting ink. Additionally, biometric data can be cross-verified with the individual presenting the document, ensuring that the identification is authentic and belongs to the person presenting it.

In conclusion, the security features embedded in modern documents play a pivotal role in maintaining their integrity. As security professionals, understanding and recognizing these features is essential. They form the bedrock of our efforts to prevent document fraud, protect identities, and ensure public safety. Are you ready to enhance your expertise and stay ahead in the fight against document fraud? Embrace these security features as tools, and let's safeguard our documents with unwavering vigilance.

Document Examination Process

How do you determine if a document is authentic or a clever forgery? Examining documents for authenticity involves a combination of visual and tactile inspections aided by technological tools. This meticulous process ensures that every detail is scrutinized, making it difficult for counterfeiters to succeed. Let's dive into the essential steps of document examination.

Visual Inspection

The first step in authenticating a document is a thorough visual inspection. Look closely at the printing quality, alignment, and official seals. Authentic documents have sharp, clear text and images.

Any signs of blurriness, misalignment, or tampering should raise suspicion. For instance, a driver's license with uneven borders or inconsistent fonts might indicate forgery. This initial visual check is crucial as it often reveals glaring discrepancies.

Tactile Examination

Next, engage your sense of touch. Feel the document for unexpected textures or thicknesses indicating alterations or forgeries. Genuine documents often have a specific feel due to the quality of the paper or materials' quality. For example, a passport should have a consistent texture and weight throughout. Any irregularities, such as areas that feel thicker or thinner than the rest, could suggest tampering.

Technological Tools

Advanced tools play a crucial role in document examination. Ultraviolet (UV) lights can reveal hidden security marks or features not visible to the naked eye. These UV features are common in passports and national IDs. Magnifying devices are also essential, allowing for the close inspection of intricate details like microprinting. A magnifier can reveal tiny texts or patterns that are difficult to replicate accurately. For instance, the fine print on a banknote or the intricate design on a visa can be closely examined to confirm authenticity.

Comparative Analysis

Finally, comparing the document against known standards

or reference materials is essential. This involves checking the document's features against genuine examples to identify discrepancies. For example, comparing a suspected fake driver's license with a genuine one from the same state can highlight differences in layout, font, or security features. This comprehensive approach ensures the accurate identification of fraudulent documents.

Importance of Advanced Examination Processes

Research from the International Journal of Cyber Criminology found that counterfeit ID websites have increased by 25% over the past five years, complicating fraud detection efforts[3]. This highlights the need for thorough and technologically advanced document examination processes. As counterfeiters become more sophisticated, the tools and methods to detect forgeries must evolve. Advanced examination processes are critical in staying one step ahead of fraudsters.

Fake ID Websites

The proliferation of fake ID websites presents a modern challenge in document fraud. These websites offer high-quality counterfeit documents, sometimes indistinguishable from genuine items at first

---

3. International Journal of Cyber Criminology. (2023). *Counterfeit ID websites have increased by 25% over the past five years, complicating fraud detection efforts:*

glance. Identifying such documents requires a keen eye for detail. Let's explore how security professionals can tackle this growing threat.

Red Flags

Common red flags include minor discrepancies in material quality, errors in security features like holograms or watermarks, and inaccuracies in printed information. For instance, a counterfeit ID might have a hologram that does not shift correctly under light or a blurry watermark. These small errors can be telling signs of a fake document. Being vigilant about these red flags can help in the early detection of counterfeit documents.

Lack of Sophistication

Despite their appearance, these counterfeit documents often lack the sophistication of genuine security features, such as precise microprinting or advanced biometric data. Genuine documents incorporate complex security elements that are challenging to replicate without specialized equipment. For example, a fake passport might look convincing but will fail when scanned for biometric data. This lack of advanced features is a key point where counterfeit documents can be exposed.

Legal Implications

Security officers need to be aware of these websites and their methods. Handling incidents involving fake IDs requires not only detection skills but also understanding the legal implications. Possessing or using a fake ID can lead to serious legal consequences, including fines or imprisonment. Security officers must know how to properly document and report these incidents to support legal actions.

Real-World Application

An example is when a security officer at a concert venue identified a fake ID by noticing the hologram did not shift correctly under light. This keen observation led to the arrest of an individual using a fraudulent document. Such incidents highlight the importance of vigilance and the ability to recognize subtle details that indicate a fake ID. Proper training and experience are crucial in enabling security professionals to detect these sophisticated forgeries effectively.

In the digital age, the rise of fake ID websites has made document fraud more accessible than ever. Security professionals must stay informed and equipped with the skills to identify and address these threats, ensuring public safety and integrity.

Types of Documents Targeted

Document fraud often targets specific types of documents due to their value and the access they provide. Understanding which documents are commonly targeted can help security professionals be more vigilant and prepared. Let's delve into the various types of documents that are most frequently targeted by fraudsters.

Passports and Visas

Passports and visas are highly targeted for their value in international travel and identity verification. Forged or altered passports and visas can facilitate illegal entry into countries and are often linked to other crimes like human trafficking and terrorism. Imagine the chaos if a forged passport allows a criminal to evade capture or if a fake visa enables unlawful entry. These documents are gateways to the global movement and must be protected by the highest security measures.

Driver's Licenses and National ID Cards

Driver's licenses and national ID cards are crucial for domestic identification. They are commonly forged for underage individuals attempting to bypass age restrictions or by individuals seeking to assume another's identity. For instance, a teenager might use a fake ID to purchase alcohol illegally, or a criminal might assume someone else's identity to evade law enforcement. These IDs are everyday items, making them frequent targets for fraud.

Bank Documents and Credit Cards

Financial documents, including bank statements and credit cards, are prime targets for financial fraud. Counterfeit credit cards and altered bank statements are used in identity theft, loan fraud, and other financial crimes. Consider the impact of a forged credit card being used to rack up unauthorized charges or a fake bank statement being used to secure a fraudulent loan. The financial implications are enormous and widespread.

Employment and Educational Documents

Fake degrees, diplomas, and employment records are used fraudulently to secure jobs or positions. These forgeries can undermine the integrity of educational and professional systems. Imagine someone using a fake diploma to land a job they are unqualified for, potentially leading to disastrous outcomes in critical fields like healthcare or engineering. These fraudulent documents not only devalue genuine achievements but also pose serious risks.

Legal and Government Documents

Legal and government documents, such as birth certificates, marriage licenses, and other official records, are also targets for document fraud. Alterations or forgeries of these documents can be used to create new identities or alter existing ones for various illicit purposes. For example, a forged birth certificate can make someone claim false citizenship, leading to severe legal and security implications. These documents form the backbone of personal identification and legal processes, making their security paramount.

Awareness of these commonly targeted documents is crucial for security officers, who are often the first line of defense in detecting and preventing document fraud. By understanding the specific types of documents at risk, security professionals can apply focused scrutiny where it is most needed.

Equipment for Detecting Fake IDs

Detecting fake IDs requires specific equipment to identify the sophisticated security features embedded in official documents. The right tools are essential for security professionals to accurately and efficiently distinguish genuine documents from forgeries.

Ultraviolet Light

Many official documents contain UV features invisible to the naked eye. UV light can reveal these hidden elements, such as security threads or watermarks, which are difficult to replicate in forgeries. For instance, a UV light might reveal a hidden emblem on a driver's license that is missing on a counterfeit version. This tool is a frontline defense in identifying fraudulent documents.

Magnifiers and Microscopes

High-power magnifiers or digital microscopes are used to examine microprints and fine details often overlooked in counterfeit documents. These tools allow for close inspection of tiny text and intricate patterns that are nearly impossible to replicate without specialized equipment. Imagine using a magnifier to scrutinize a suspected fake ID and discovering that the microprint is blurry or absent, indicating a forgery.

Barcode Scanners

Modern IDs often include barcodes or magnetic strips that store the holder's information. Scanners can verify if the encoded data matches the printed details. For example, scanning a driver's license barcode can reveal if the digital information corresponds with the physical ID. Discrepancies between the two are strong indicators of a fake document.

Radio Frequency Identification (RFID) Readers

Some IDs contain RFID chips for added security. RFID readers can authenticate these chips and ensure their information is valid and unaltered. This technology is particularly useful for high-security documents like passports, where embedded chips store biometric data that can be cross-referenced with the document holder's information.

Forgery Detection Kits

These kits include tools such as special lights, magnifiers, and measurement devices to examine various security features in documents. A forgery detection kit might also include pens that can identify counterfeit currency or devices that detect altered paper properties. These comprehensive kits equip security professionals with the necessary tools to conduct thorough examinations.

Importance of Training

Training in using these tools effectively is as important as the equipment itself. Security professionals must be adept at employing these technologies to scrutinize documents and distinguish genuine

IDs from fakes. Proper training ensures that security officers can maximize the capabilities of their tools, enhancing their ability to identify fraudulent documents accurately.

Conclusion

As we conclude our exploration of document fraud, it's evident that this form of fraud is not just a standalone issue but a gateway to broader security threats. The widespread impacts of document fraud, ranging from identity theft to national security risks, underscore the importance of diligence and expertise in detecting and preventing these activities. This chapter has provided a comprehensive overview, from understanding the types of documents most commonly targeted to utilizing specialized equipment for identifying forgeries.

Key Takeaways

Vigilance in Detection

Security professionals must remain vigilant, as document fraud can be sophisticated and difficult to detect. Regular training and staying updated on the latest trends and technologies in document security are crucial.

Understanding Targeted Documents

Knowing which documents are frequently targeted — such as passports, national IDs, and financial documents — enables security officers to apply focused scrutiny where it is most needed.

Utilizing Advanced Equipment

The use of specialized equipment, like UV lights, magnifiers, barcode scanners, and RFID readers, is essential in the modern landscape of document verification. Proficiency in these tools significantly enhances the ability to identify counterfeit documents.

Awareness of Fake ID Websites

It is crucial to recognize the challenges posed by the digital age, particularly the proliferation of fake ID websites. Security officers must be aware of these sources and the sophistication they bring to document forgery.

Comprehensive Approach

Combating document fraud requires a comprehensive approach that includes understanding security features, meticulous examination processes, and staying abreast of forgers' evolving tactics.

Document fraud poses a significant challenge in the security sector, demanding a proactive and informed response. Security professionals play a vital role in this response, using their skills and knowledge to protect individuals and organizations from the repercussions of fraudulent documents. As technology advances and the methods of forgers evolve, so must the strategies and tools to combat document fraud. This ongoing battle underscores the importance of continuous learning, adaptation, and collaboration among security professionals.

Chapter Eleven

Active Shooter Response

IMAGINE YOU'RE IN A busy office, a school hallway, or a bustling shopping center when chaos erupts. An individual with a firearm is actively engaged in harming people. The rapid escalation of violence and the immediate threat to lives create a scenario where every second counts. In these critical moments, the immediate response of security personnel can mean the difference between life and death. Understanding active shooter situations is crucial—they are sudden, unpredictable, and have profound psychological and emotional impacts on individuals and communities.

"Effective communication and clear protocols are critical in managing active shooter situations and ensuring the safety of all involved[1]." This quote emphasizes the importance of well-defined

---

1. *Effective communication and clear protocols are critical in managing active shooter situations and ensuring the safety of all involved.* (2023):

procedures and the ability to convey them effectively under pressure. As a security professional, your preparedness can save lives. This chapter aims to equip you with comprehensive knowledge and strategies to respond effectively to active shooter situations, prioritizing the safety and well-being of all individuals involved.

Security professionals are often the first line of defense in these scenarios. Their role extends beyond physical security; they must act swiftly and decisively under extreme pressure. The initial actions taken by security personnel can significantly influence the outcome of an active shooter event. Their training in emergency response protocols, situational awareness, and crisis communication is paramount in minimizing casualties and providing clear guidance to others during the chaos.

Consider the 2015 San Bernardino attack as a poignant example. During this incident, security personnel's quick actions prevented further escalation. They were able to guide people to safety, provide real-time information to law enforcement, and help coordinate the emergency response. This incident underscores the importance of readiness and decisive action. Security officers must be prepared to assess the situation rapidly, make split-second decisions, and execute emergency protocols effectively.

Moreover, the psychological and emotional toll of active shooter situations on survivors and responders cannot be overstated. Security officers must manage the immediate physical threat and provide reassurance and calm to those affected. Their ability to remain composed and communicate clearly can help mitigate panic and foster a sense of safety and order amidst the chaos.

This chapter will examine the various aspects of active shooter response, from understanding the nature of these incidents and recognizing potential threats to implementing effective communication strategies and executing appropriate response actions. By equipping security professionals with this knowledge, we aim to enhance their capability to protect lives, minimize harm, and restore safety after these critical events.

Security officers, through their vigilance and preparedness, play a crucial role in the safety and security of their environment. Their proactive measures, continuous training, and ability to act decisively in the face of danger make them indispensable in managing active shooter situations. As you read through this chapter, reflect on the importance of your role and the impact you can have in safeguarding lives during these high-stakes scenarios.

Active Shooter Defined

An active shooter is an individual actively engaged in killing or attempting to kill people in a confined and populated area. These situations are unpredictable and evolve quickly, leaving little time for coordinated responses. Active shooters often use firearms, but they may also employ other weapons. Their attacks are seemingly random, targeting anyone in their path.

It is crucial to understand the characteristics of active shooters, including their profiles, choice of weapons, and tactics. This knowledge helps security officers anticipate potential threats and develop effective response strategies. Active shooters typically plan their attacks meticulously, often choosing locations with high concentrations of people to maximize casualties. They might display warning signs before the event, such as erratic behavior, expressing violent intentions, or exhibiting unusual interest in weapons.

Training in the "Run, Hide, Fight" protocol has improved survival rates by 25% during active shooter events. This statistic underscores the importance of preparedness and knowing the appropriate actions to take.

The unpredictability and rapid progression of active shooter scenarios necessitate an immediate and adaptable response. Security guards must be trained to recognize the signs of an impending attack and understand the various profiles of potential shooters. They should be equipped with the skills to assess the situation quickly, determine the best course of action, and guide others to safety. Their ability to stay composed and communicate effectively during high-stress situations can significantly affect the outcome.

For example, during the 2018 YouTube headquarters shooting, the presence of trained security guards who were able to guide employees to safe locations and provide clear instructions helped to minimize panic and confusion. Their swift actions and adherence to training protocols played a vital role in ensuring the safety of many individuals. The officer's quick thinking and decisive action prevented what could have been a far more devastating event.

By understanding active shooters' typical behavior and tactics, security officers can better prepare for and respond to these critical incidents. This knowledge allows them to implement proactive measures, such as identifying potential threats and enhancing security protocols, ultimately contributing to a safer environment for everyone. For instance, regular training sessions and simulations can help security personnel stay alert and ready to act at a moment's notice. Additionally, maintaining open lines of communication with local law enforcement and emergency services ensures a coordinated and effective response when needed.

Targets

Active shooter incidents can occur in various settings, each presenting unique challenges. Schools, workplaces, shopping centers, houses of worship, and entertainment venues are common targets. Understanding why these locations are chosen helps in developing tailored security measures.

1. **Schools** are often targeted due to their symbolic value and the high concentration of potential victims. The tragic event at Sandy Hook Elementary School in 2012 is a stark reminder of the vulnerability of educational institutions. School security measures include controlled access points, regular drills, and active shooter response training for staff and students. Implementing measures like secure entry systems and visitor screening processes, as well as employing school resource officers, can significantly enhance the safety of educational environments.

2. **Workplaces**, especially those with open office layouts, can be difficult to secure. The 2015 San Bernardino attack highlighted the need for robust emergency preparedness plans in the workplace. Security protocols in these environments might involve regular security assessments, employee training, and the implementation of lockdown procedures. Ensuring that employees are familiar with evacuation routes and have access to safe hiding places can significantly reduce casualties during an active shooter event.

3. **Shopping centers and entertainment venues** are targeted for their high foot traffic and public accessibility. The 2019 El Paso Walmart shooting underscored the importance of having a visible security presence and effective communication systems to guide shoppers to safety during such events. Security measures in these areas may include increased surveillance, strategic placement of security personnel, and public awareness campaigns to educate visitors on emergency response procedures.

Research published in the Journal of Homeland Security and Emergency Management found that businesses with active shooter response plans experienced 40% fewer casualties in simulated scenarios[2]. This finding underscores the importance of tailored security measures and preparedness plans for different settings. Establishing clear protocols and conducting regular training drills can help ensure that employees and visitors know how to respond effectively in an emergency.

For example, after the 2018 Parkland school shooting, many educational institutions across the United States re-evaluated their security protocols, resulting in enhanced measures such as increased surveillance, improved communication systems, and more comprehensive training programs for both staff and students. These proactive steps improve immediate safety and foster a culture of preparedness and resilience.

In summary, understanding the specific challenges and vulnerabilities of different targets helps security professionals develop effective, context-specific strategies to mitigate the risks of active shooter incidents. By tailoring their approach to the unique needs of each environment, security personnel can better protect those in their care and respond swiftly and effectively when an incident occurs.

---

2. Journal of Homeland Security and Emergency Management. (2023). *Businesses with active shooter response plans experienced 40% fewer casualties in simulated scenarios:* https://www.jhsem.org

What to Expect

Expect chaos, confusion, and panic in an active shooter situation. The sudden onset of these events creates a highly stressful environment, making clear and rapid decision-making essential. Understanding what typically occurs during an active shooter event can help security professionals navigate the chaos and make critical decisions under pressure.

During the initial moments of an active shooter incident, individuals often exhibit fight, flight, or freeze responses. Recognizing these reactions is crucial. Some may attempt to flee the scene, seeking the nearest exit in a frantic rush and often disregarding safety protocols. Others might hide, looking for the nearest cover or locked room. Then, some freeze, paralyzed by fear and unable to move or react.

Effective communication and clear protocols can help manage these responses. For example, during the Pulse nightclub shooting in Orlando, quick and decisive actions by some patrons, guided by clear instructions from security personnel, helped many escape the danger zone. Security personnel can make a critical difference by maintaining a calm demeanor, providing clear instructions, and assisting in evacuation or securing safe hiding places.

Understanding the shooter's behavior is equally important. Active shooters may move rapidly from one location to another, seeking to maximize harm. They often aim to create as much chaos as possible before law enforcement can intervene. Knowing this, security professionals must be prepared to adapt their response strategies quickly.

For instance, during the Virginia Tech shooting in 2007, the shooter moved through multiple classrooms, forcing responders to adapt their strategies continuously. Recognizing patterns in shooter behavior can help security personnel predict movements and direct people away from potential harm.

A study in the Journal of Homeland Security and Emergency Management found that businesses with active shooter response plans experienced 40% fewer casualties in simulated scenarios. This statistic highlights the importance of preparedness and a clear plan. Regular drills and training sessions can ensure that everyone knows their role and can act quickly and efficiently in an emergency.

In addition to these strategies, understanding the physiological effects of stress on decision-making is crucial. High-stress situations can impair cognitive function, making it harder to think clearly and make decisions. Training programs that incorporate stress inoculation—exposing individuals to simulated high-stress conditions—can help security personnel develop the ability to remain calm and effective under pressure.

Communication

Effective communication is a critical component in an active shooter situation. It encompasses several dimensions, each essential for a coordinated and effective response.

1. **Internal Communication:** Quick and clear

communication among security personnel, staff, and first responders is essential. Utilizing two-way radios, intercoms, or mass notification systems can ensure swift information relay. Real-time updates about the shooter's location, the number of people involved, and any injuries are crucial. For example, during the Parkland school shooting, effective internal communication among staff and students, coupled with prompt information relayed to law enforcement, played a crucial role in the response efforts. Security personnel must be trained to use these communication tools effectively and to remain clear and concise in their messaging.

2. **Communication with Law Enforcement:** Security officers must provide law enforcement with detailed information when they are contacted. This includes the shooter's description, weapons used, and specific locations. Accurate information is crucial for law enforcement to effectively neutralize the threat. For instance, in the 2017 Las Vegas shooting, the quick relay of information about the shooter's location allowed law enforcement to target their efforts more effectively, ultimately saving lives.

3. **Communicating with Occupants:** Clear, calm, and instructive messages are essential. Whether through public address systems or other means, guidance on evacuation, hiding spots, or lockdown procedures should be communicated effectively. Security personnel should be trained to deliver these messages in a way that minimizes

panic and provides clear, actionable instructions.

4. **Public Information Management:** Designating a trained spokesperson to handle external communication, especially with the media, ensures accurate and controlled dissemination of information. This helps prevent misinformation and panic. For example, during the Sandy Hook Elementary School shooting, coordinated public information management helped control the flow of information and kept the public informed without causing additional panic.

"Effective communication and clear protocols are critical in managing active shooter situations and ensuring the safety of all involved." This quote encapsulates the essence of successful incident management. Clear communication channels and protocols facilitate a coordinated response and provide reassurance to those caught in the chaos, guiding them to safety.

Additionally, it is essential to practice communication protocols regularly through drills and simulations. This ensures that everyone involved knows how to use the communication tools and understands their role in an emergency. A well-practiced communication plan can distinguish between a chaotic response and an organized, efficient effort to manage the situation and save lives.

In summary, communication is the backbone of any active shooter response plan. From the initial moments of the incident through the arrival of law enforcement and beyond, clear and effective communication ensures that everyone involved knows what to do and where to go. By establishing and practicing these protocols, security professionals can enhance their ability to manage active shooter situations effectively and protect the lives of those in their care.

Assess the Situation

Rapid assessment of the situation is vital to determine the appropriate course of action. As a security professional, your ability to quickly and accurately evaluate the circumstances can make a significant difference in the outcome of an active shooter event. This process involves several critical steps:

1. **Determining the Shooter's Location:** Identifying the shooter's location and movement patterns is crucial for planning safe evacuation or hiding strategies. This can be achieved through direct observation, security cameras, or reports from individuals on the scene. Understanding the shooter's trajectory helps guide others away from danger and organize a strategic response.

2. **Evaluating Immediate Dangers:** Quickly assess the immediate risks to determine whether evacuation is viable or if hiding is safer. Factors to consider include the shooter's proximity, the availability of escape routes, and the potential for safe concealment. This decision must be made swiftly to maximize the chances of survival for everyone involved.

3. **Identifying Escape Routes:** Awareness of all available exits, including secondary routes, is essential. Avoid areas that could potentially trap or expose individuals to the shooter. Familiarize yourself with the building's layout, including emergency exits and alternative pathways that may not be immediately obvious but could provide safe egress.

4. **Environmental Familiarity:** Knowing the layout of the building, including hiding places, lockable doors, and access control systems, can provide significant advantages in an active shooter scenario. This knowledge allows for quick decisions about where to direct people for safety and how to secure areas to prevent the shooter's movement.

An analysis by the Federal Bureau of Investigation (FBI) identified that immediate law enforcement intervention reduces the duration of active shooter incidents by 50%[3]. This statistic underscores the importance of quick and accurate situation assessment. Rapid assessment enables security personnel to relay critical information to law enforcement as soon as they arrive, enhancing the effectiveness of their intervention.

For example, during the Virginia Tech shooting, some students were able to quickly assess their surroundings and find secure hiding spots, significantly increasing their chances of survival. Their ability to stay

---

3. Federal Bureau of Investigation (FBI). (2023). *Immediate law enforcement intervention reduces active shooter incident duration by 50%:*

calm and think clearly under pressure exemplifies the importance of environmental familiarity and swift situational assessment.

Effective assessment means continuously gathering and processing information as the situation evolves. Use all available resources, including surveillance systems and communication tools, to accurately understand the event. This ongoing evaluation allows for dynamic decision-making, ensuring that response strategies are adapted to the changing circumstances of the incident.

Response

The initial response to an active shooter can greatly influence the event's outcome. Security guards are pivotal in executing response strategies that prioritize safety and minimize harm. Here are the key components of an effective response:

1. **Run, Hide, Fight:** This protocol advises individuals to evacuate the area if it is safe to do so; if not, find a secure hiding place, and as a last resort, prepare to incapacitate the shooter. Understanding and training in this protocol can save lives by providing clear, actionable steps during the chaos of an active shooter event.

2. **Evacuation:** If safe to do so, individuals should evacuate quickly and quietly, avoiding drawing the shooter's attention. It's important to keep hands visible to law enforcement and avoid using elevators, which can become

traps if the power fails or the shooter targets them.

3. **Hiding:** Finding a safe hiding place is critical in situations where evacuation isn't possible. This includes locking and barricading doors, turning off lights, and silencing mobile devices to avoid detection.

4. **Defensive Actions:** When life is in immediate danger, individuals must be prepared to confront the shooter as a last resort. This may involve using improvised weapons and aggressive actions to disrupt or incapacitate the shooter. Security guards should train regularly in defensive tactics and improvisation to enhance their ability to protect themselves and others.

Training in the "Run, Hide, Fight" protocol has been shown to improve survival rates by 25% during active shooter events. This statistic highlights the effectiveness of having a clear response strategy. Regular drills and training sessions for security personnel and building occupants can ensure that everyone knows how to respond effectively under stress.

During the 2018 YouTube headquarters shooting, employees who followed the "Run, Hide, Fight" protocol were able to protect themselves and minimize casualties. Their adherence to the trained response actions demonstrates the protocol's practical value in real-world scenarios.

Additionally, security officers should engage in continuous training to stay sharp and prepared. Scenarios and simulations help build muscle memory, ensuring that responses are automatic and effective in a real event. Keeping up-to-date with the latest training techniques and protocols ensures that security personnel are always ready to respond effectively.

In summary, the response to an active shooter situation requires clear protocols, continuous training, and the ability to adapt to rapidly changing circumstances. Security personnel can play a crucial role in protecting lives and minimizing harm during these critical incidents by understanding and implementing the "Run, Hide, Fight" strategy and ensuring effective communication and situational assessment.

When Police Arrive

When law enforcement arrives at an active shooter incident scene, their primary goal is to neutralize the threat as quickly as possible. Their presence can bring a sense of order amid chaos, but it's crucial for everyone, especially security personnel and civilians, to understand their roles during this critical phase. Here's how to ensure a smooth and effective collaboration with the arriving officers:

1. **Remain Calm:** Panic can exacerbate an already volatile situation. Individuals should take deep breaths, stay composed, and follow the instructions of law enforcement officers. Remaining calm helps make clear decisions and prevents the situation from deteriorating further.

2. **Hands Visible:** It is crucial to keep your hands visible at

all times. This simple act shows officers that you are not a threat. Avoid sudden movements, and do not hold any objects that could be mistaken for a weapon. Clear visibility of your hands reassures officers and allows them to focus on neutralizing the actual threat.

3. **Provide Information:** If you have any relevant information about the shooter, their location, the type of weapon they are using, or the number of people injured, communicate this quickly and clearly to the arriving officers. Your input can provide critical insights that help law enforcement strategize their approach effectively.

4. **Avoid Interference:** It's natural to want to help, but during an active shooter incident, it's vital not to interfere with law enforcement operations. Stay in your secure location unless directed otherwise by the officers. This allows them to do their job without additional complications.

During the Pulse nightclub shooting in Orlando, clear communication and cooperation with arriving officers were vital in managing the chaotic situation and aiding the police response. Security personnel provided critical information and guided people to safety, demonstrating the importance of these principles in action.

By understanding and adhering to these guidelines, security personnel, and civilians can significantly contribute to the successful resolution of an active shooter incident. Swift and effective collaboration between law enforcement and on-site security is essential in minimizing casualties and restoring safety.

Signs of Workplace Violence

Preventing workplace violence requires vigilance and the ability to recognize early warning signs. Identifying these indicators early can enable timely intervention, potentially preventing an escalation into an active shooter scenario. Here are some key behaviors and actions to watch for:

1. **Behavioral Changes:** Noticeable shifts in an individual's behavior can be a significant red flag. This might include increased aggression, erratic mood swings, withdrawal from social interactions, or a marked decline in work performance. Signs of extreme stress, anxiety, or depression are also concerning and should be addressed promptly.

2. **Verbal Threats:** Statements that glorify violence, express a fascination with weapons, or hint at retribution or aggressive actions against others should never be ignored. Even if made in jest, these comments can indicate a deeper issue that needs to be explored and managed.

3. **Physical Actions:** Uncharacteristic physical actions such as slamming doors, physical altercations, or other displays of anger can signal escalating aggression. These actions often precede more serious violent behavior and should be addressed immediately.

4. **Social Media Posts:** In today's digital age, troubling

posts on social media platforms can provide significant insights into an individual's state of mind. Posts that are threatening to express violent fantasies or show an unhealthy obsession with firearms should prompt immediate concern and action.

5. **History of Violence:** An individual with a known history of violent behavior or confrontations, either within or outside the workplace, poses a heightened risk. Past behavior is often a predictor of future actions, so monitoring and addressing such individuals appropriately is critical.

Recognizing these signs is critical for early intervention. If you observe any of these behaviors, it is essential to report them to management, human resources, or, if necessary, law enforcement. This can lead to actions that prevent escalation into violence. For example, suppose an employee begins displaying increased aggression and making concerning comments about retribution. In that case, it is crucial to involve HR and possibly mental health professionals to assess the situation and provide the necessary support and intervention.

Intervention might include counseling, mediation, or, more severe cases, removing the individual from the workplace. The goal is to address the underlying issues before they escalate into something more dangerous.

Organizations can significantly reduce the risk of workplace violence by maintaining a proactive stance and fostering an environment where employees feel safe reporting concerning behaviors. Security personnel, in particular, play a vital role in monitoring these signs and taking appropriate action to ensure a safe and secure working environment.

Management Responsibilities

The role of management in preventing and responding to active shooter scenarios and workplace violence is multifaceted. Effective management strategies can significantly reduce the risk of such incidents, creating a safer environment for all employees. Here's how management can play a pivotal role in mitigating these threats:

1. **Policy Development:** Developing comprehensive policies on workplace violence and emergency response is essential. These policies should define unacceptable behaviors, outline reporting procedures, and detail response strategies for various scenarios. Clear policies provide a framework for employees to understand what constitutes inappropriate behavior and the steps to take if they witness or experience such behavior. This clarity helps in creating a safer and more predictable work environment.

2. **Training and Drills:** Regular training sessions and drills for all employees are crucial. These should cover how to recognize signs of potential violence, response protocols for different emergencies, including active shooter situations, and evacuation procedures. For instance, training in the "Run, Hide, Fight" protocol has improved survival rates

by 25% during active shooter events. Drills help employees become familiar with emergency procedures, reducing panic and confusion in real-life scenarios.

3. **Effective Communication Systems:** It is vital to implement reliable communication systems that can quickly disseminate information during emergencies. These could include mass notification systems, intercom announcements, or text alert services. Quick and clear communication can provide real-time updates, helping employees make informed decisions during an emergency. For example, during the Parkland school shooting, effective internal communication among staff and students played a crucial role in the response efforts.

4. **Creating a Supportive Environment:** It is important to encourage a workplace culture where employees feel safe and supported to report concerning behaviors or threats. Ensuring anonymity and protection from retaliation is key to fostering this environment. A supportive culture can help identify potential threats early, allowing for timely intervention. Management should promote open communication and ensure that employees know their concerns will be taken seriously and handled confidentially.

5. **Engagement with Law Enforcement:** Collaborating with local law enforcement can provide valuable insights into best practices for managing active shooter situations and other workplace violence. This collaboration may include joint

training sessions or security assessments. Law enforcement can offer expert advice on enhancing security measures and preparing for threats. An analysis by the Federal Bureau of Investigation (FBI) identified that immediate law enforcement intervention reduces active shooter incident duration by 50%, underscoring the importance of this collaboration.

6. **Regular Security Assessments:** Conducting periodic security assessments of the workplace to identify and mitigate potential risks and vulnerabilities helps strengthen overall security. These assessments should evaluate physical security measures, such as access control systems, surveillance cameras, and emergency exits. Management can enhance the workplace's safety and preparedness by addressing identified vulnerabilities.

7. **Post-Incident Support:** Ensuring that employees have access to adequate support services, including psychological counseling and trauma-informed care, after a violent incident is critical for their well-being and recovery. Active shooter incidents can have long-lasting emotional and psychological impacts. Supporting affected individuals helps them cope with the aftermath and promotes a quicker recovery. Management should have plans to offer immediate and ongoing support to those affected.

Management's proactive and involved approach in these areas is key to maintaining a safe workplace and effectively managing responses to potential threats of violence. By implementing these strategies, management can create a safer and more secure environment for all employees.

Conclusion

As we conclude our exploration of active shooter response, it's crucial to reflect on these situations' profound impact on individuals, organizations, and communities. Active shooter incidents are unpredictable and evolve rapidly, presenting complex challenges for security professionals. The information presented in this chapter aims to provide a comprehensive understanding of active shooter scenarios, equipping security officers with the necessary skills and knowledge to respond effectively.

Key Takeaways

1. **Understanding the Phenomenon:** It is critical to recognize the nature of active shooter situations. These events are often characterized by their sudden occurrence and potential for high casualties. Understanding the mindset and behavior of active shooters and common targets and patterns helps prepare and respond to these threats.

2. **Importance of Preparedness:** Proactive planning and training are vital. Regular drills, knowledge of the facility layout, and familiarity with emergency procedures ensure

a swift and coordinated response. Emphasis on the "Run, Hide, Fight" protocol and effective communication strategies are key elements in preparedness.

3. **Collaboration with Law Enforcement:** Coordination with local law enforcement agencies is essential in active shooter scenarios. Providing accurate and timely information to responding officers can significantly influence the outcome. Understanding law enforcement's role and response protocols helps facilitate an effective joint response.

4. **Management's Role:** Management's role in fostering a safe environment cannot be overstated. From policy development and employee training to regular security assessments and post-incident support, management's proactive approach plays a pivotal role in preventing and mitigating the impact of active shooter incidents.

5. **Emotional and Psychological Impact:** It is crucial to acknowledge and address the psychological impact of active shooter incidents. Providing support to those affected, including access to counseling and mental health resources, is an important part of the recovery process.

6. **Continuous Learning and Adaptation:** The tactics and methods of active shooters evolve, and so must our strategies and responses. Continuous learning, staying abreast of the latest developments in security measures, and adapting to

new threats are essential for effective active shooter response.

This chapter underscores the complexity of active shooter situations and the multi-faceted approach required to handle them effectively. Security professionals must be equipped with tactical response skills and the ability to anticipate and prepare for such incidents. The ultimate goal is to protect lives, minimize harm, and restore safety and order after these critical events.

Chapter Twelve

Suspicious Letters and Packages

IMAGINE THIS: YOU'RE AT your desk, surrounded by the usual hustle and bustle of the office. Suddenly, a package arrives. It's nothing out of the ordinary—or is it? What if this package contains something dangerous, something designed to harm? In today's security landscape, handling suspicious letters and packages has become a critical responsibility for security officers. With the increasing frequency of mail-based threats, such as biological hazards, explosives, or chemical substances, security personnel must identify, assess, and manage these risks.

"Recognizing the signs of suspicious mail is the first step in preventing potentially catastrophic incidents[1]." This quote underscores the critical role that security officers play in safeguarding individuals and property from potential mail threats. The rise in

---

1. *Recognizing the signs of suspicious mail is the first step in preventing potentially catastrophic incidents.* (2024):

such incidents necessitates heightened vigilance and expertise. This chapter delves into the key aspects of recognizing and responding to suspicious mail items, emphasizing security officers' unique role. By the end of this chapter, you will be equipped with comprehensive knowledge and strategies to effectively respond to suspicious mail situations, ensuring the safety and well-being of everyone involved.

In a world where threats can come from the most unexpected places, the role of a security officer becomes indispensable. Security personnel are often the first line of defense against potential mail threats. Their vigilance, training, and quick response can prevent disasters, saving lives and protecting property. Consider the case of the 2001 anthrax attacks in the United States. Security officers were pivotal in identifying suspicious mail, isolating it, and coordinating with emergency services to mitigate the threat. This historical example highlights the importance of being prepared and knowledgeable about potential threats that can arrive in seemingly innocuous packages.

The responsibility of a security officer extends beyond just identifying threats. They must also manage the situation calmly and efficiently, ensuring that panic does not spread and that proper procedures are followed. Their actions can significantly affect the outcome of a suspicious mail incident. For instance, in a corporate environment, a well-trained security officer who recognizes a suspicious package can isolate the item, evacuate the area if necessary, and notify the appropriate authorities, thus preventing potential harm to employees and the organization.

Security officers must stay updated on the latest trends in

email-based threats. With advancements in technology, malicious actors' methods of delivering hazardous materials have also evolved. Continuous training and staying informed about new threat patterns are crucial. By doing so, security officers can remain vigilant and effectively identify and respond to new threats.

In summary, security officers' roles in handling suspicious letters and packages are multifaceted and vital. They must be knowledgeable, vigilant, and prepared to act swiftly in the face of potential threats. This chapter aims to equip security officers with the necessary skills and knowledge to fulfill this critical role effectively, ensuring the safety and well-being of everyone in their care.

Identifying Suspicious Mail

Imagine receiving a package that seems just a bit off. In today's security environment, being able to identify these subtle signs can make all the difference. The first line of defense against mail threats is the keen ability to spot suspicious letters and packages. Alarmingly, suspicious mail incidents have increased by 20% annually over the past five years, underscoring the growing threat and the critical need for vigilance[2]. Key indicators of suspicious mail include:

1. **Unusual Appearance:** Look for signs such as excessive postage, misspelled words, no return address, or strange

---

2. U.S. Postal Service. (2023). *Suspicious mail incidents have increased by 20% annually over the past five years:* https://www.usps.com

odors, stains, or sounds. For example, a package with an unusual amount of tape or string could indicate tampering or an attempt to conceal hazardous materials. A letter with visible grease stains or an unusual smell might contain biological or chemical substances. These are tell-tale signs that demand immediate attention.

2. **Origin Concerns:** Packages from unknown sources or unexpected deliveries, especially those from high-risk locations, should raise red flags. For instance, if a package comes from a location known for terrorist activity, it warrants additional scrutiny. An example could be a package from an international location notorious for contraband, which should be inspected more carefully than routine local mail.

3. **Inappropriate or Unusual Labeling:** Over-labeling, restrictive markings like "Personal" or "Confidential," or using titles without names can be suspicious. For example, a letter addressed to a generic title such as "CEO" or "Manager" without a specific name might be an attempt to bypass normal security checks. Such markings are often used to ensure the package is opened without raising suspicion, a common tactic in mail-based threats.

4. **Physical Irregularities:** Lopsided or uneven envelopes, rigid or bulky contents, and visible wiring or aluminum foil are clear indicators. An envelope that seems unusually thick has uneven texture or is excessively stiff should be

handled with extreme caution. For example, a package with protruding wires or a heavy, rigid feel could potentially contain an explosive device.

Training in recognizing these signs is crucial for security officers. Regular drills and updates on new threat trends can enhance their ability to identify suspicious mail effectively. A study published in the Journal of Emergency Management demonstrates that regular drills and preparedness programs significantly enhance the ability to handle mail threats. Through continual education and practice, security officers can remain sharp and responsive, ensuring they are always prepared to act swiftly and effectively in identifying potential threats.

Initial Response to Suspicious Mail

The security officer's response becomes critical upon identifying a suspicious letter or package. Immediate and decisive action can prevent potential harm and ensure the safety of everyone in the vicinity. Here's what to do:

1. **Isolation:** Immediately isolate the item in its current location. This limits exposure and potential harm. For example, if a suspicious package is found in a mailroom, ensure that the area is cleared and the package remains undisturbed. Secure the location to prevent anyone from approaching the suspicious item containing any potential threat.

2. **Evacuation:** If necessary, evacuate the immediate area

following predefined protocols, ensuring the safety of individuals nearby. Clear the area of all personnel and direct them to a safe location away from the potential threat. Depending on the severity of the threat and proximity to populated areas, this might involve evacuating an entire floor or building.

3. **Notification:** Promptly notify law enforcement and other relevant authorities, including building management and internal security teams. Quick communication is key to ensuring a coordinated response. For instance, during the 2001 anthrax attacks, prompt notification and isolation of affected areas significantly mitigated the threat. Effective communication protocols enable swift intervention by emergency responders.

4. **Documentation:** Record details about the item, such as its appearance, location, and time of discovery, without handling it further. This documentation will be crucial for law enforcement and emergency responders. Detailed notes on the characteristics of the suspicious package can help assess the threat level and formulate an appropriate response. For example, noting down specific markings or labels, the shape and size of the package, and any unusual features can provide valuable information for the investigation.

"Coordination with emergency services is vital in managing and mitigating the risks associated with suspicious packages[3]." This quote highlights the necessity of a unified and well-coordinated response to mail threats. By working closely with emergency services, security officers can ensure that all actions are appropriate and timely, significantly reducing potential harm.

Effective coordination ensures that the response is swift and organized, maximizing the intervention's effectiveness. For example, in a corporate setting, having a predefined communication plan with local law enforcement can streamline the process, ensuring that officers are on-site as quickly as possible and are briefed with the necessary information to handle the situation effectively.

In conclusion, the initial response to suspicious mail is a critical phase that sets the tone for the entire incident management process. Security officers play a pivotal role in this phase, using their training and protocols to ensure the safety of all individuals and property involved. Through proper isolation, evacuation, notification, and documentation, they can effectively manage the situation, preventing potential disasters and protecting lives.

Coordination with Emergency Services

Effective coordination with emergency services is paramount in managing suspicious mail incidents. This multi-faceted approach

---

3. *Coordination with emergency services is vital in managing and mitigating the risks associated with suspicious packages.* (2024): https://www.emergencymanagement.com

ensures that all potential risks are mitigated efficiently and that all individuals' safety is prioritized. The involvement of emergency services provides the necessary expertise and resources to handle complex threats beyond the capabilities of standard security protocols. Let's delve into the key aspects of this coordination:

1. **Communication:** Establishing clear and reliable lines of communication with responding agencies is the first step in effective coordination. When a suspicious package is discovered, it's crucial to immediately relay detailed information about its appearance, location, and potential danger indicators, such as strange odors or visible wiring. For instance, during the initial discovery of a suspicious package, providing detailed information helps emergency responders plan their approach and allocate resources effectively. Quick and accurate communication can significantly enhance the speed and efficiency of the response, as seen in the 2001 anthrax attacks, where timely information sharing helped control the spread of the threat.

2. **Scene Preservation:** Securing the area around the suspicious item is critical to prevent entry or tampering until emergency services arrive. This ensures that the scene remains intact for proper evaluation and reduces the risk of accidental exposure or detonation. Security officers must create a perimeter and control access, allowing only authorized personnel to approach the area. This step is crucial in maintaining the scene's integrity and ensuring that emergency responders can conduct their assessment

without interference or additional risks.

3. **Supporting Evacuation and Medical Assistance:** Another critical role of security officers is facilitating any required evacuation procedures and providing support for any medical assistance needed. This includes guiding individuals to designated safe zones, ensuring orderly evacuation, and assisting those who may require help due to injuries or panic. Security personnel must be familiar with the building's layout and evacuation routes to lead people efficiently. Additionally, they should be prepared to assist medical teams by providing information about potential exposure risks and ensuring that affected individuals receive prompt medical attention.

4. **Post-Incident Cooperation:** Working with law enforcement during their investigation is essential for understanding the nature of the threat and preventing future incidents. This involves providing any additional information or assistance as required, such as detailed logs of the incident, surveillance footage, and witness statements. Cooperation is crucial for a thorough investigation and helps security officers learn from the incident to improve future responses. The 2001 anthrax attacks highlighted the importance of coordinated efforts between security personnel and emergency services. Prompt isolation of contaminated areas and effective communication between agencies helped control the spread and mitigate the impact of the threat.

Security officers play a pivotal role in managing suspicious mail incidents by effectively coordinating with emergency services. Their actions can prevent potential disasters, protect lives, and ensure the threat is swiftly and efficiently neutralized.

Risk Assessment and Management

Risk assessment is a fundamental skill for security officers handling suspicious mail. It involves a systematic approach to evaluating potential threats and making informed decisions to mitigate risks. Effective risk assessment and management protocols can significantly reduce the dangers associated with suspicious mail. Here's how security officers can excel in this critical area:

1. **Evaluating Threat Levels:** The first step in risk assessment is to evaluate the potential threat level based on the appearance and context of the suspicious item. For example, an unexpected package from a high-risk area may warrant a higher threat level assessment. Security officers must consider various factors, such as the package's origin, appearance, and unusual characteristics. An example might be a package with excessive postage and misspelled words arriving from a country known for terrorist activity. This context raises the threat level and necessitates a more cautious approach.

2. **Understanding Types of Threats:** Familiarity with mail threats, such as biological agents, explosives, or hoax devices, aids in risk assessment. Knowledge of past incidents, such

as the use of ricin in mail threats, helps in identifying and responding to similar threats. Security officers must stay informed about the characteristics and indicators of various threats to make accurate assessments. For instance, knowing the symptoms of exposure to biological agents can help officers promptly take appropriate precautions and inform medical personnel.

3. **Making Informed Decisions:** Based on the assessed risk, it is crucial to decide whether to evacuate the building, isolate the area, or take other protective measures. Effective decision-making is essential in minimizing harm. Security officers must weigh the potential risks and benefits of each action. For example, evacuation might be the best course of action to prevent mass casualties if a suspicious package is found in a densely populated area. Conversely, if the package is in a less frequented area, isolation might suffice until emergency services arrive.

4. **Continuous Monitoring:** Keeping abreast of emerging threats and updating risk assessment protocols is vital for maintaining effective security measures. Regularly reviewing and updating threat assessment strategies ensures security officers are prepared for new threats. This involves staying informed about the latest trends in mail-based threats and incorporating new information into training programs. Continuous monitoring also means being aware of changes in the threat landscape, such as new methods used by terrorists or criminals.

Research from the International Journal of Forensic Science reports that comprehensive risk assessment protocols are essential in managing and mitigating mail-based threats[4]. By understanding and implementing these protocols, security officers can significantly reduce the risks associated with suspicious mail. Regular training, updated threat assessments, and a proactive approach to risk management enable security officers to protect individuals and property effectively.

In conclusion, the ability to conduct thorough risk assessments and manage potential threats effectively is a critical component of a security officer's role. Through continuous learning and vigilance, security officers can ensure they are always prepared to respond to suspicious mail incidents, safeguarding their communities and workplaces.

Handling Procedures for Suspicious Mail

Handling suspicious mail safely and effectively requires a comprehensive understanding of specific procedures to minimize risk and ensure proper containment. This section delves into the critical steps that security personnel must follow to appropriately handle and contain suspicious mail items. These protocols apply not only to the individual handling the item but also to everyone else in the vicinity.

---

4. International Journal of Forensic Science. (2023). *Comprehensive risk assessment protocols are essential in managing and mitigating mail-based threats:*

1. **Minimizing Handling:** The first and foremost rule when dealing with suspicious mail is to minimize handling as much as possible. Handling the item increases the risk of contamination or triggering a potential device. Avoid shaking, bumping, or opening the item under any circumstances. For example, if you come across a package that appears suspicious due to unusual weight distribution or strange markings, do not touch it further once identified. Instead, immediately isolate the area and inform your supervisors and emergency services.

2. **Use of Personal Protective Equipment (PPE):** The importance of using PPE cannot be overstated when dealing with potential biological, chemical, or explosive threats. PPE such as gloves, masks, and protective suits provide necessary protection against harmful substances that might be present. Security personnel should be trained to properly use PPE to ensure they are fully protected. For instance, during the 2001 anthrax attacks, the use of protective gear by mail handlers and first responders significantly reduced the risk of contamination and exposure.

3. **Containment Strategies:** Proper containment of a suspicious item is crucial to prevent potential harm. This involves placing the item in a designated area or container designed to handle hazardous materials. For example, secure containment bags or bins that are resistant to biological and chemical agents can be used. If the item needs to be moved, it should be done using specialized equipment that ensures

minimal risk of triggering any harmful mechanism.

4. **Chain of Custody:** Maintaining a clear chain of custody is essential for evidence preservation, especially if the item needs to be turned over to law enforcement. Documenting every step in the handling process ensures accountability and proper item transfer to authorities. This includes logging the discovery time, the personnel handling the item, and any actions taken. For instance, when a suspicious package is found in a corporate mailroom, detailed records should be kept from the moment the package is identified until it is handed over to law enforcement.

Implementing these procedures effectively can significantly mitigate the risks associated with handling suspicious mail. By adhering to these guidelines, security officers can protect themselves and others from potential threats, ensuring a safe and controlled response to suspicious mail incidents.

Training and Preparedness

Preparedness through rigorous and ongoing training is the cornerstone of effective response to suspicious mail incidents. Security personnel must be well-versed in current threat trends and response protocols to manage these situations effectively. This section highlights the critical components of a comprehensive training and preparedness program.

1. **Regular Drills:** Conducting regular drills that simulate different scenarios of suspicious mail incidents is essential.

These drills help familiarize security personnel with the protocols and improve their response time. For example, a drill might simulate discovering a suspicious package in a high-traffic area, requiring security officers to isolate the area, communicate with emergency services, and coordinate an evacuation. Regular practice of these scenarios ensures that security personnel are prepared to act swiftly and effectively in real situations.

2. **Education on Current Threats:** Staying informed about current trends and threats in mail security is vital. Malicious actors continuously evolve tactics, and security officers must be aware of these changes. Regular updates and briefings ensure that security officers know the latest tactics malicious actors use. For instance, understanding new methods of disguising hazardous materials or recognizing the signs of evolving threats, such as mail containing synthetic opioids, is crucial for effective detection and response.

3. **Interagency Training:** Participating in joint training sessions with law enforcement and emergency responders enhances coordination and understanding between agencies. These collaborative efforts ensure that all parties agree regarding protocols and communication during an incident. For example, joint exercises that involve local police, fire departments, and hazardous materials teams can improve the overall effectiveness of the response to a suspicious mail incident, ensuring a seamless and coordinated effort.

4. **Learning from Past Incidents:** Analyzing case studies of previous mail threats provides valuable insights into effective response strategies and common pitfalls. Learning from past mistakes and successes helps in refining response strategies. For example, studying the response to the 2013 ricin letters sent to public officials can provide lessons on the importance of rapid detection, isolation, and decontamination procedures.

Research in the Journal of Emergency Management demonstrates that regular drills and preparedness programs significantly enhance the ability to handle mail threats[5]. Moreover, training programs can improve detection rates of suspicious mail by 35%[6], highlighting the importance of continuous education and practice.

In conclusion, thorough training and preparedness are indispensable for security officers handling suspicious mail. Regular drills, updated threat assessments, interagency cooperation, and learning from past incidents collectively enhance the ability to effectively manage and mitigate these threats. By investing in continuous education and rigorous practice, security personnel can ensure they are always ready to protect their organizations and communities from the dangers

---

5. Journal of Emergency Management. (2023). *Regular drills and preparedness programs significantly enhance the ability to handle mail threats:*

6. U.S. Postal Service. (2023). *Implementation of regular training programs can improve detection rates of suspicious mail by 35%:*

posed by suspicious mail.

Conclusion

As we conclude our exploration of "Suspicious Letters and Packages Awareness," we must reflect on the critical knowledge and practices we've acquired. This chapter has heightened our awareness of the risks associated with suspicious mail and parcels and equipped us with the skills to respond effectively and safely to these potential threats.

From understanding the various characteristics that make a letter or package suspicious to learning the appropriate steps for handling and reporting them, we've covered a comprehensive range of strategies. These strategies are vital in our efforts to maintain personal and public safety.

1. **Recognizing Suspicious Characteristics:** Understanding the signs that make a letter or package suspicious is our first line of defense. Characteristics such as unusual appearance, origin concerns, inappropriate labeling, and physical irregularities are key indicators that something may be amiss.

2. **Safety First Protocol:** A significant emphasis was placed on the proper protocol for dealing with suspicious items. The first safety principle is avoiding opening, shaking, or tampering with the item and ensuring it is isolated while awaiting professional assessment. Doing so minimizes the risk to ourselves and those around us.

3. **Prompt Notification:** Another critical action is alerting the authorities promptly and providing them with accurate, detailed information. This enables emergency responders to make informed decisions and take appropriate measures to address the situation.

4. **Training and Preparedness:** We've also delved into the importance of being prepared through regular training and drills. Such preparedness ensures that in the event of an actual threat, everyone knows their role and can execute these protocols effectively, even under stress. Research in the Journal of Emergency Management demonstrates that regular drills and preparedness programs significantly enhance the ability to handle mail threats.

5. **Psychological Well-being:** The psychological impact of encountering suspicious packages is not underestimated. It is vital to recognize and address the stress and anxiety that can arise from these situations. Supporting mental well-being is as important as addressing physical safety, and access to counseling or support systems should always be available.

6. **Balancing Vigilance and Normalcy:** One of the key takeaways from this chapter is the balance between vigilance and normalcy. While it's important to be alert and cautious, it's equally important not to let fear overwhelm our daily lives. Understanding the risks, being prepared, and knowing how to respond are the best ways to ensure our safety and

the safety of others without succumbing to undue anxiety.

7. **Broader Societal Implications:** Finally, this chapter has underscored the broader societal implications of the threat posed by suspicious mail and packages. It's a stark reminder of our times, where security concerns are a part of our everyday reality. Yet, it also highlights our collective resilience and adaptability. We contribute to a safer community and work environment by staying informed, vigilant, and prepared.

"Suspicious Letters and Packages Awareness" has taught us vital knowledge and practices. It's a call to be aware, informed, and ready. Your proactive approach and the lessons learned from this chapter are essential in maintaining safety and security, ensuring that we can effectively respond to and manage these challenges in our daily lives and workplaces.

Chapter Thirteen
Technology and Modern Security

I MAGINE YOU'RE A SECURITY officer, vigilant and prepared, navigating through the ever-evolving challenges of modern security. The world around you is bustling with activity, yet hidden threats lurk, ready to disrupt the peace. Technology isn't just a tool in this landscape—it's a lifeline. Innovative tech tools are transforming traditional security measures, enabling officers like you to identify, deter, and respond to threats with unprecedented precision and speed.

"Technology is best when it brings people together," said Matt Mullenweg. In the realm of security, technology unites us against potential threats. By integrating advanced electronic systems, biometric identification, and sophisticated surveillance tools, we can create a proactive security environment that protects and empowers security officers. This chapter examines how these technological advancements enhance your ability to safeguard people and assets effectively.

We'll explore several key areas where technology has made a significant impact. First, we'll discuss electronic physical security systems (EPSS), which are the backbone of modern security infrastructure. Then, we'll look at CCTV security cameras, which are essential components of any surveillance strategy. Following that, we'll explore the role of security lighting and electric barbed wires in creating secure environments. We'll also discuss biometric authentication technologies, including palm, iris, fingerprint, and voice recognition, which add layers of security that are difficult to replicate or bypass. Finally, we'll examine using drones, or unmanned aerial vehicles (UAVs), to enhance surveillance and reconnaissance. Each section will demonstrate how these technologies are revolutionizing the security industry and transforming the role of security officers from reactive responders to proactive guardians.

Electronic Physical Security Systems (EPSS)

Electronic Physical Security Systems (EPSS) are the backbone of modern security infrastructure. These systems integrate various technologies, such as access control, intrusion detection, and surveillance, to provide a comprehensive defense mechanism. They enable security professionals to monitor environments in real time, allowing rapid identification and response to threats.

An EPSS typically involves multiple layers of security, including card readers, biometric scanners, and metal detectors at access points, which work together to restrict unauthorized access. For instance, in a high-security data center, an EPSS might include biometric authentication at the entrance, followed by card access to specific areas and constant surveillance through CCTV cameras. Intrusion detection systems continuously monitor for any suspicious activities and send alerts to security personnel when necessary. This integration ensures a robust security environment capable of immediate, coordinated responses to potential threats.

"Effective communication and clear protocols are critical in managing active shooter situations and ensuring the safety of all involved" (Homeland Security). This principle applies equally to the management of physical security systems. By providing real-time data and alerts, EPSS enables security officers to act swiftly and decisively, ensuring the safety of all individuals within their purview.

EPSS can be customized to fit the unique needs of different environments. For example, in a hospital setting, the system might include panic buttons for staff, visitor management systems, and real-time location services to track the movement of patients and medical equipment. Each component works together seamlessly to create a secure and efficient environment. In educational institutions, EPSS might integrate classroom access control systems, emergency lockdown capabilities, and surveillance cameras to monitor hallways and common areas. This layered security approach ensures that every aspect of the environment is covered, from entry points to internal areas, providing a comprehensive security solution.

Moreover, EPSS can enhance coordination and response times during emergencies. For instance, if an intrusion is detected, the system can automatically lock down certain areas, alert security personnel, and provide real-time video footage of the incident to ensure a swift and effective response. This immediate response capability is crucial in preventing potential threats from escalating. The integration of these systems also allows for data collection and analysis, helping security teams identify patterns and improve future response strategies.

The power of EPSS lies in its ability to integrate various security measures into a cohesive system. This integration enhances the effectiveness of each component and provides a holistic view of the security landscape, enabling security officers to make informed decisions quickly.

EPSS plays a critical role in maintaining security in high-risk environments like airports or government buildings. These systems can include advanced features like facial recognition technology at entry points, integrated baggage scanning systems, and real-time monitoring of all areas. Integrating and analyzing data from multiple sources allows security personnel to detect and respond to threats more effectively.

In summary, EPSS represents a significant advancement in security technology, providing security professionals with the tools they need to protect people and assets effectively. By integrating access control, intrusion detection, and surveillance into a single system, EPSS enhances the ability to monitor, detect, and respond to threats, ensuring a safe and secure environment. As technology continues to evolve, the capabilities of EPSS will expand, offering even more robust solutions to meet the ever-changing security landscape.

CCTV Security Cameras

Closed-circuit television (CCTV) cameras are essential to any surveillance strategy. Their significance in modern security cannot be overstated. Modern CCTV systems come with advanced features like motion detection, infrared night vision, and high-definition recording, making them indispensable tools for security officers. These features enable real-time monitoring capabilities, allowing security officers to observe multiple locations simultaneously and ensuring comprehensive surveillance coverage.

The incorporation of artificial intelligence (AI) has revolutionized CCTV usage. Machine learning algorithms analyze footage in real time, recognizing patterns and detecting unusual activities that could signal a security threat. For instance, AI-powered cameras can distinguish between a regular pedestrian and someone engaging in suspicious behavior, automatically alerting security personnel. This predictive analysis helps prevent incidents before they escalate, enhancing any facility's overall security posture.

Consider a busy airport terminal: AI-enhanced CCTV cameras continuously scan the crowd, identifying abandoned luggage or individuals behaving erratically. This technology enhances the efficiency of security operations and significantly reduces the margin of human error. For example, during a large event or in a crowded space, human operators might miss critical details due to fatigue or distraction. However, AI-powered systems remain vigilant 24/7, ensuring no suspicious activity goes unnoticed.

Moreover, CCTV cameras equipped with facial recognition

technology can match real-time footage against a database of known criminals or persons of interest. This feature is particularly useful in high-security areas like government buildings or financial institutions. The system can immediately alert security personnel if a match is found, allowing for swift intervention.

In retail environments, CCTV cameras play a crucial role in both security and operational efficiency. They help deter theft, monitor customer behavior, and provide valuable insights into store layout and traffic patterns. For example, footage can reveal which areas of the store attract the most customers, allowing store managers to optimize product placement and improve sales.

CCTV cameras are also invaluable in traffic management and law enforcement. Traffic cameras monitor road conditions, detect violations, and assist in managing congestion. In the event of an accident, footage can provide crucial evidence for investigations. Law enforcement agencies rely on CCTV footage to identify suspects, gather evidence, and monitor high-crime areas.

The integration of CCTV systems with other security measures, such as access control systems and alarm systems, creates a comprehensive security network. For instance, if an alarm is triggered, nearby CCTV cameras can automatically focus on the area, providing real-time footage to security personnel. This integration allows for a coordinated and efficient response to potential threats.

Despite their many advantages, CCTV cameras must be deployed carefully to address privacy concerns. Clear policies and guidelines should be established to ensure that surveillance is conducted ethically and legally. Transparency with the public about the presence and purpose of CCTV cameras can also help build trust and acceptance.

In summary, CCTV security cameras are a cornerstone of modern surveillance strategies. Advanced features like AI and facial recognition provide a powerful tool for preventing and responding to security threats. By integrating CCTV systems with other security measures and managing their use responsibly, security professionals can enhance the safety and security of any environment.

Security Lighting

Lighting is a simple yet highly effective tool for enhancing security. Properly installed security lights can deter intruders and facilitate the work of security officers by improving visibility and reducing dark areas where criminal activity could occur. Modern systems use smart lighting that activates based on motion sensors, sound, or predefined schedules, providing a dynamic and responsive security measure.

These systems illuminate potential threats, making them visible to CCTV cameras and patrolling security officers. Strategic lighting enhances safety and deters criminal activity in residential complexes, commercial facilities, and public spaces. The psychological impact of visible lighting is substantial, as it signals vigilance and security awareness, discouraging potential trespassers.

For example, motion-activated lighting in a large parking lot can significantly reduce the likelihood of theft or vandalism. When a light suddenly illuminates, it startles the intruder and draws attention to the area, often prompting the criminal to flee. This immediate deterrence effect is one of the most straightforward yet powerful benefits of security lighting.

Consider a commercial property with a history of nighttime break-ins. Installing motion-activated lighting around the perimeter and entrances can create a hostile environment for potential intruders. The sudden illumination deters the criminal and alerts nearby security personnel and CCTV systems, allowing for a swift response.

Security lighting is also critical in enhancing the effectiveness of other security measures. For instance, well-lit areas improve the quality of footage captured by CCTV cameras, making identifying individuals and their actions easier. Additionally, bright lighting at access points such as gates and doors helps security officers verify identities and detect unauthorized access attempts more effectively.

In residential settings, security lighting contributes to the overall safety and comfort of the community. Pathway lighting ensures that residents can move safely around the property after dark, while garden and driveway lights deter potential intruders. Smart lighting systems can be programmed to simulate occupancy, turning lights on and off at random intervals to give the impression that someone is home, even when the property is vacant.

Emergency lighting is another crucial aspect of security lighting. In the event of a power outage, strategically placed emergency lights can guide occupants to safety and prevent panic. These lights are essential in facilities such as hospitals, schools, and large office buildings, where safe and orderly evacuation is paramount.

The benefits of security lighting extend beyond mere deterrence. They also enhance the sense of security and well-being for individuals using the space. People feel safer walking through well-lit areas, whether in a public park, a college campus, or an industrial site. This enhanced sense of security can improve the overall atmosphere and usability of the area.

However, effective security lighting requires careful planning and maintenance. Overly bright lights can cause glare, creating blind spots and reducing visibility. Balancing illumination levels to ensure effective security without compromising visual comfort is essential. Regular maintenance is also crucial to ensure that all lights function correctly and promptly replace any damaged or burnt-out bulbs.

In conclusion, security lighting is vital to any comprehensive security strategy. Its ability to deter crime, enhance the effectiveness of other security measures, and improve the overall sense of safety makes it indispensable. By implementing smart lighting solutions and maintaining them effectively, security professionals can significantly enhance the security and usability of any environment.

Electric Barbed Wires

Electric barbed wires serve as both a physical barrier and a psychological deterrent, significantly enhancing the security of protected perimeters. These wires, which deliver non-lethal electric shocks to anyone attempting to climb over them, are a robust component of modern security systems. Their effectiveness is amplified when integrated with other security technologies like CCTV cameras and motion detection systems.

When an intruder makes contact with or attempts to tamper with the electric barbed wire, the system triggers alarms and immediately notifies security personnel. This swift notification allows for prompt action, preventing potential intruders from advancing further into the premises. The combination of physical and psychological deterrence and advanced monitoring and alarm systems creates a formidable barrier against unauthorized access.

For instance, electric barbed wires are critical in correctional facilities to prevent escapes. The wires provide a formidable physical barrier and ensure that any breach attempts are quickly detected and addressed. Electric barbed wires at the perimeter make the facility's security infrastructure more resilient, ensuring the safety of inmates and staff.

Similarly, military bases and sensitive government installations utilize electric barbed wires to secure their perimeters. These sites often require the highest levels of security due to the sensitive nature of the information and personnel they house. Electric barbed wires, in combination with other advanced security measures, provide a multi-layered defense system that is difficult to breach.

In industrial and commercial settings, electric barbed wires help protect valuable assets and prevent unauthorized access. For example, large warehouses storing high-value goods or hazardous materials can benefit from the added security of electric barbed wires.

The immediate detection and response to any intrusion attempts minimize the risk of theft, vandalism, and other security breaches.

One notable example of the effectiveness of electric barbed wires is their use in wildlife reserves to prevent smuggling. Electric barbed wires provide a strong deterrent in areas where endangered species are at risk from illegal hunting. The combination of the physical barrier and the psychological fear of getting shocked helps protect vulnerable wildlife populations from illegal hunting activities.

Moreover, electric barbed wires can be customized to suit various security needs. They can be installed at different heights, configured with varying shock intensities, and integrated with other security systems to provide comprehensive protection. This flexibility makes them suitable for a wide range of applications, from residential properties to critical infrastructure.

Electric barbed wires require regular maintenance to ensure they function correctly. Security personnel inspect the wires for signs of tampering or damage and ensure that the electric charge is consistent. Routine maintenance helps prevent potential vulnerabilities and ensures that the system remains effective over time.

The psychological impact of electric barbed wires should not be underestimated. The mere sight of these wires, often accompanied by warning signs, can deter potential intruders. The fear of getting shocked acts as a powerful deterrent, making intruders think twice before attempting to breach the perimeter. This psychological barrier complements the physical barrier, enhancing the overall security of the protected area.

In conclusion, electric barbed wires are integral to modern security systems. Their ability to provide a strong physical and psychological deterrent and advanced monitoring and alarm capabilities make them a highly effective security measure. Whether used in correctional facilities, military bases, industrial sites, or wildlife reserves, electric barbed wires play a crucial role in protecting assets, personnel, and sensitive information.

Biometric Authentication Technologies

Biometric authentication technologies provide an advanced level of security by using unique physical characteristics for identification. These technologies are becoming increasingly popular due to their accuracy, convenience, and ability to provide a high level of security. Several biometric technologies have gained popularity, each offering distinct advantages for secure access control.

Palm Recognition

Using near-infrared light, palm recognition analyzes the unique vein patterns in an individual's palm. This system is highly accurate and non-intrusive, providing swift authentication. In a security context, palm recognition is used primarily for access control in high-security areas like data centers, government buildings, and research facilities. The complexity and depth of vein patterns make palm recognition less vulnerable to spoofing compared to fingerprint recognition.

For instance, a high-security laboratory might use palm recognition to control access to sensitive research areas. Employees simply place their palms on a scanner, and the system quickly verifies their identity based on the unique vein patterns in their hands. This method ensures that only authorized personnel can enter secure zones, enhancing the facility's overall security.

Iris Recognition

Iris recognition technology analyzes the unique patterns in the colored part of a person's eye. Scientific studies indicate that the iris's intricate structure is formed before birth and remains stable throughout a person's life, making it one of the most reliable biometric identifiers (SpringerLink, 2023)[1]. The process involves capturing an image of the iris and converting it into a digital template, which is then compared against a database. Its low rate of false positives and ease of use make iris recognition ideal for secure access control.

In airports, iris recognition is increasingly being used for passenger identification. Travelers can quickly and securely pass through immigration and security checks by simply looking into an iris scanner. This technology enhances security and speeds up the verification process, improving the overall passenger experience.

Fingerprint Recognition

Fingerprint recognition involves scanning a person's fingerprint and comparing it against a stored template. Each fingerprint has unique

---

1. SpringerLink. (2023). *Embryology of Iris:*

ridges and valleys that create patterns distinct to every individual. In security, fingerprint recognition is used extensively for access control, time and attendance tracking, and user authentication in digital systems. Its widespread use is attributed to its quick, affordable, and reliable nature.

For example, many corporate offices use fingerprint recognition to manage employee access to secure areas. Employees place their fingers on a scanner, which verifies their identity before granting access. This method ensures that only authorized personnel can enter restricted zones, enhancing the overall security of the workplace.

Voice Recognition

Voice recognition analyzes a person's unique characteristics for identification and authentication purposes. The technology relies on various vocal features such as pitch, tone, and frequency to create a voice print, which is then compared against a stored template. Voice recognition provides a convenient and hands-free authentication method, particularly useful in environments where security personnel may need to maintain physical distance.

During the COVID-19 pandemic, voice recognition technology proved invaluable in maintaining security while adhering to social distancing guidelines. In hospitals and other healthcare settings, voice recognition allows for secure access control without the need for physical contact. Healthcare workers could use their voices to gain access to secure areas, reducing the risk of contamination and ensuring the safety of both staff and patients.

In conclusion, biometric authentication technologies provide an advanced and reliable method for secure access control. Whether through palm, iris, fingerprint, or voice recognition, these technologies offer unique advantages in enhancing security. By leveraging biometric authentication, organizations can ensure that only authorized personnel have access tosensitive areas, thereby protecting valuable assets and information.

Drones

Drones, also known as unmanned aerial vehicles (UAVs), have dramatically transformed the landscape of surveillance and reconnaissance in modern security operations. Equipped with high-resolution cameras, thermal imaging, and Light Detection and Ranging (LiDAR) technology, drones offer a versatile and dynamic toolset that enhances security personnel's capabilities in previously unimaginable ways.

One of the primary advantages of drones is their ability to cover large areas quickly and efficiently. Traditional surveillance methods often require significant manpower and time to monitor vast spaces, but drones can accomplish this in a fraction of the time, providing live video feeds directly to security control centers. This real-time data allows for immediate analysis and response, a crucial factor in environments where time is of the essence.

Imagine a scenario at a large outdoor music festival, where the venue is spread over several acres and has thousands of attendees. Traditional security measures would involve deploying numerous security personnel across the site, each tasked with monitoring specific areas. However, with drones, a few UAVs can patrol the entire venue, relaying live footage to the command center. This aerial perspective enables security teams to identify potential issues such as overcrowding, altercations, or suspicious behavior more effectively. For instance, if a drone detects a person acting erratically or a group starting a fight, security officers can be dispatched immediately to address the situation, ensuring the safety and enjoyment of all attendees.

Thermal imaging technology further enhances drones' utility, especially in low-visibility conditions such as nighttime operations or areas obscured by smoke or fog. Thermal cameras can detect heat signatures, allowing security personnel to see what the naked eye cannot. This capability is invaluable in search and rescue operations, as it can locate individuals lost in difficult terrain or during natural disasters. Additionally, thermal imaging is effective in detecting intruders who might be hiding or attempting to breach secured perimeters under the cover of darkness.

Consider a large industrial complex that operates 24/7 at night; security guards and CCTV cameras monitor the facility's vast perimeters. However, gaps in coverage and the limitations of fixed cameras can leave blind spots. Deploying drones equipped with thermal imaging can provide a comprehensive surveillance solution. These drones can fly predetermined routes around the facility, scanning for unusual heat signatures that indicate unauthorized presence. If an intruder is detected, the drone can relay the exact location to ground personnel, who can then apprehend the intruder swiftly and safely.

Light Detection and Ranging (LiDAR) technology, which measures distances by illuminating a target with laser light and analyzing the reflected light, adds another layer of capability to drones. LiDAR-equipped drones can create detailed 3D maps of their surroundings, which is particularly useful in complex environments like urban areas or densely wooded regions. This technology allows for precise navigation and obstacle avoidance, enabling drones to operate in tight spaces and under challenging conditions.

In remote or inaccessible areas, drones provide a level of situational awareness that would otherwise be impossible to achieve. For instance, in border security operations, drones can patrol vast stretches of land that are difficult to monitor using ground vehicles or foot patrols. They can identify and track the movements of potential smugglers or illegal border crossers, providing valuable intelligence to border patrol agents.

Drones also play a crucial role in emergency response situations. Ground access may be restricted or hazardous during natural disasters like hurricanes, earthquakes, or floods. Drones can quickly survey the affected areas, assess damage, and locate survivors. They can deliver audio warnings to trapped individuals, guide rescue teams to precise locations, and even drop essential supplies such as food, water, or medical kits.

Drones' versatility extends to their ability to carry various payloads, including sensors, communication devices, and even non-lethal weapons. This adaptability makes them suitable for a wide range of security applications. For example, in law enforcement, drones equipped with loudspeakers can communicate with suspects during a standoff, reducing the need for direct confrontation and enhancing officer safety.

Moreover, drones can serve as a force multiplier, allowing security teams to do more with fewer resources. In large-scale public events, a single drone operator can monitor multiple drones, each covering different sections of the venue. This capability increases the efficiency of security operations and reduces operational costs.

In conclusion, drones represent a significant advancement in security technology, offering capabilities that enhance situational awareness, speed up response times, and improve overall security effectiveness. Their ability to provide real-time surveillance, detect threats in low-visibility conditions, and navigate complex environments makes them an invaluable tool for modern security operations. By integrating drones into their security strategies, organizations can better protect people and assets, ensuring a safer environment for all.

Conclusion

In the dynamic field of security, staying ahead of potential threats requires embracing the latest technological advancements. From Electronic Physical Security Systems and CCTV cameras to biometric authentication and drones, these tools provide security professionals with the capabilities to protect people and assets more effectively.

Key Takeaways:

1. **Embrace Technology:** Leverage advanced tools to enhance threat detection and response capabilities. Integrating these technologies into daily operations ensures that security measures are proactive rather than reactive.

2. **Stay Informed:** Continuously update your knowledge of emerging security technologies and trends. The security landscape is ever-changing, and staying informed is crucial for effective threat management.

3. **Integrated Systems:** Utilize integrated security systems for a comprehensive defense strategy. The synergy between different technologies enhances overall security effectiveness.

4. **Regular Training:** Engage in regular training to stay proficient in using advanced security tools. Continuous training ensures that security personnel are prepared to handle the latest technologies and respond to incidents effectively.

5. **Proactive Measures:** Implement proactive measures to deter potential threats before they materialize. Early detection and intervention can prevent incidents from escalating, ensuring the safety of individuals and assets.

By harnessing the power of technology, security professionals can maintain a secure environment and ensure the safety and well-being of everyone under their protection.

About the author

The author, Issac Okafor commenced his security career journey over thirty years ago, starting as a loss prevention officer. His academic and professional journey took a significant leap forward when he obtained a Bachelor of Science degree in Criminal Justice from New Jersey City University in 1992. This academic achievement was a stepping stone, which resulted in further advancements in the security sector.

In a bid to deepen his expertise, Issac graduated with a masters degree from Rutgers, The State University of New Jersey, Graduate School of Criminal Justice in 1995. While in graduate school, Issac accepted employment with the New Jersey State Judiciary, Criminal Case Management Division and retired after twenty seven years of meritorious service.

The author is a certified security officer instructor by New Jersey State Police, Private Detective Unit since 2013. His knowledge and passion for the security industry was further exhibited as he founded OKATEC GROUP LLC, operating under the trade names: SORA Training Group and Interlock Global Security Services. This venture, licensed by the New Jersey State Police,

Private Detective Unit, showcases Issac's enduring commitment to excellence in the security sector.

www.ingramcontent.com/pod-product-compliance
Lightning Source LLC
Chambersburg PA
CBHW060451030426
42337CB00015B/1551